DATE DUE

Open Learning Courses for Adults

A MODEL OF STUDENT PROGRESS

David Kember

Educational Technology Publications
Englewood Cliffs, New Jersey 07632

Library of Congress Cataloging-in-Publication Data

Kember, David.
　Open learning courses for adults : a model of student progress /
David Kember.
　　p.　cm.
　Includes bibliographical references and indexes.
　ISBN 0-87778-280-6
　1. Distance education. 2. Adult education. 3. Motivation in
education. 4. Instructional systems--Design. I. Title.
LC5800.K46 1995
374'.13--dc20　　　　　　　　　　　　　　　　　　　　94-21399
　　　　　　　　　　　　　　　　　　　　　　　　　　　CIP

Printed in the United States of America.

Library of Congress Catalog Card Number:
94-21399.

International Standard Book Number:
0-87778-280-6.

First Printing: January, 1995.

Acknowledgments

I have been an active researcher in the area of student progress and attrition from distance education and open learning courses since the early eighties. This book draws upon most of my research during this period. It is an attempt to reinterpret all of the large amount of data I have gathered over this period in the light of the insights I have progressively gained.

I am, therefore, deeply indebted to my various co-workers during this period. I would like to thank Greg Harper, my partner in a project which examined the approaches to learning of distance education students in Australia. I owe a great debt to my colleagues in the Hong Kong distance learning project: Tammy Lai, David Murphy, Irene Siaw, Julianne Wong and K.S. Yuen. I must also thank the Hong Kong Polytechnic for supplying funding for this project.

I am grateful to the academic staff and administrators who cooperated by allowing myself and my co-workers to put their courses under scrutiny. I would also like to thank the large number of busy students who gave their time to complete questionnaires and respond to interviews. Without their frank and detailed comments it would have been impossible to compile such a graphic picture of the life of an open learning student.

Four leading researchers in the field of distance education: Cheryl Amundsen, Connie Dillon, Mavis Kelly and David Murphy were kind enough to read through an earlier version of the text and each made valuable suggestions for improving it. I would also like to thank Lawrence Lipsitz, the Editor at Educational Technology Publications, for some worthwhile comments and for his efforts to remove errors, improve consistency, and enhance readability.

I am indebted to Monica Yeung for the superb graphics which are an important feature of the book.

I acknowledge the permission of Professors Noel Entwistle and Paul Ramsden for permission to reproduce selected items from the Approaches to Studying Inventory.

Figure 3-1 is from Tinto, V. (1975). Drop-out from higher education: a theoretical synthesis of recent research. *Review of Educational Research, 45*(1), 89-125. It is copyright (1975) by the American Educational Research Association and is adapted by permission of the publisher.

The interview schedule and Distance Education Student Progress inventory reproduced in Appendices A and B are © David Kember, Tammy Lai, David Murphy, Irene Siaw and K.S. Yuen, except for items adapted from the Approaches to Studying Inventory. They are reproduced with the permission of Tammy Lai, David Murphy, Irene Siaw and K.S. Yuen.

Table of Contents

Foreword

Distance education is a rapidly growing field with respect to both practice and promise. With respect to practice, distance education has permeated all sectors of education, ranging from primary school to higher education to business and industry, within just a few short years. With respect to promise, it is a field which may redefine 21st century education. The growing impact of distance education is significant given the fact that the field is but in its infancy. Even the defining term, distance education has been in use only a few short years. With rapid advances in technology we can only imagine what future decades will hold for our institutions of learning.

Within this backdrop, David Kember brings us his book *Open Learning Courses for Adults: A Model of Student Progress*. This book is an important contribution to both the practice and to the study of distance education. This work pulls together in a single conceptual model, the many diverse elements of the field of distance education. Unlike much of the existing research in the field, this model serves to help us explain the interrelationships among learners and their context, learning and instruction, organization and context, and culture and policy.

For the practitioner the book provides conceptually grounded recommendations for both policy and practice which link the principles of instructional design and the provision of learner support. Rarely are these two important elements of distance education addressed within a single model. In addition, David Kember's research also identifies practical approaches to the design of instruction which can be used to meet the needs of learners with differing styles of learning. His research on deep and surface learning translates into specific recommendations for both course design and learner support.

The model of student progress is based upon sound theoretical constructs and the application of a series of qualitative and quantitative studies. Although, the focus of the work is upon open learning settings, the model holds the potential to further our understanding of all distance learning formats and delivery systems. We at the University of Oklahoma are using this model as a basis for a series of studies on progress of students enrolled in telecourses. We also are using the model to explore the issue of social integration and culture which we hope will provide insight into the participation and progress of our increasingly culturally diverse student population.

The book makes a significant contribution to the field of distance education, and provides a basis for grounding future contributions. The theoretical framework is well grounded in the work of Tinto, which David Kember adapts to the adult distance student based upon a series of both quantitative and qualitative studies. The model potentially serves as an organizing framework for future theoretical development in the field of distance education, by conceptually linking theories which relate the psychological factors, socio-political factors, organizational factors, and instructional factors.

It is a valuable book for all those concerned with the practice and study of distance education. Everyone who is involved with distance education, and every individual who develops or teaches classes in distance education will find this book an important addition to their library.

Connie L. Dillon

**Associate Professor of Adult and Higher Education
The University of Oklahoma**

Preview

A Model of Student Progress in Open Learning Courses

This book proposes a model of student persistence in open learning and distance education courses for part-time adult students. The book is divided into four parts.

Part A   *Background Theory*

The scope of the book is defined by examining definitions of open and distance learning. The characteristics of adult students are examined. The various routes by which open learning students can start but not finish a course are then examined. The theoretical origins of the model, drawn from both on-campus and distance education, are discussed. It is proposed that modifications to existing models are necessary if they are to be appropriate for adult students studying at a distance.

Part B   *Illustration and Explanation of the Model*

The outlines of a new model are proposed and the elements of it are explained and illustrated part-by-part using quotations from student interviews and case studies. Initial components of the linear model refer to the entry characteristics of students. Intervening components address the issue of integrating study demands into the academic and social environments. The model also has a cost/benefit analysis and a recycling loop.

Part C   *Quantitative Tests of the Model*

The results are presented from a quantitative test of the full
model drawn from a sample of students in three courses. A
subsequent replication study repeated the test on three further
courses.

Part D   *Implications for Policy and Practice*

Implications of the model for enhancing course completion and
improving academic outcomes are discussed. The first chapter in
this part deals with implications for the instructional design of
courses. The next draws conclusions for tutoring and student
support services. Strategies are then suggested for counseling
students on integrating study demands with work, family and
social commitments. The final chapter considers general
implications of the model and makes suggestions for further
research.

Conceptual Framework

A diagrammatic representation of the full model is shown below.
This diagram is used as a conceptual framework to facilitate
access and aid understanding of the book. The model is
developed, explained, and illustrated, and implications are
drawn, component-by-component. There is a synopsis at the
beginning of each chapter. From the fourth chapter onwards, the
synopsis includes a diagram of the relevant element from the
complete model, showing the topic to be covered and its
relationship to the model as a whole.

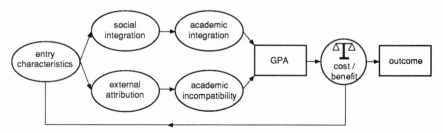

GPA and outcome measures are shown as rectangles. Main
components of the model are shown in ovals. Each of the

components have sub-components or sub-scales. These are shown as rectangles branching out from the main component, when the sub-components are relevant to a particular chapter.

Part A

Background Theory

Chapter 1

Adult Students in Open and Distance Learning Courses

Synopsis

This chapter defines the scope of the book. The characteristics of open learning and distance education courses are discussed. In terms of the way distance education courses are offered, the most important characteristic of such courses is the fact that the teachers and learners are physically separated for much of the time.

A characterization of open learning courses is proposed which incorporates elements related to the removal of participation barriers and others derived from the assumptions of andragogy from adult learning theory.

The students enrolled in the courses are normally mature adults studying part-time. The students, therefore, still retain their commitments to work, family and social lives. This dual existence can markedly distinguish them from full-time on-campus students who can have a more focused relationship with academic life. This significant dual role is, though, shared by adult students in a variety of other courses, suggesting that many of the findings from this work could have wide applicability in adult education.

Open and Distance Learning

From the title of this book it should be clear that it is concerned with adult students enrolled in open learning courses. The term open learning is commonly interpreted very broadly to encompass a wide variety of types of course. Such courses are also given numerous alternative titles, which are either seen as synonyms for open learning or regarded as a sub-set of it. The book is, therefore, also about distance education, telecourses, flexistudy, correspondence education, external study, resource-based training and an ever growing list of alternative names.

The intention of the book is to propose, develop, test and draw implications from a model of student progress which will be applicable to adults studying part-time in courses of these types. I propose to largely restrict myself to using the terms open learning and distance education, which seem to be the ones most commonly used. Hopefully the reader will be able to mentally substitute appropriate local or currently fashionable terminology.

The aim is to produce a model which will be generic to a diverse range of courses. The model may, therefore, need some degree of adaptation to suit particular courses or local conditions. The key concepts and main components of the model should, though, be generally applicable so minor adaptation should be straightforward.

As I intend to use the terms distance education and open learning, I will start by discussing their attributed meanings, starting with distance education, the historically older term.

Distance Education

Distance education can trace its genesis to correspondence education. Correspondence schools have traditionally offered an education consisting of two components: a printed study booklet and a number of written interactions between tutor and student, based around assignments. The term "correspondence education" became inappropriate when some institutions, such as the Open University in the United Kingdom, started offering an environment of educational experiences too rich to be adequately described in that way.

Even in distance education courses with the most varied of educational environments, the various elements can usually still be classified into two aspects that are analogous to those of traditional correspondence education. Study materials are generally made available by the institution for the learners, and assistance is afforded through a range of support services. Study materials may be classified by the distinguishing feature that they are often pre-prepared and are normally either delivered or transmitted to the student. The study materials can incorporate a variety of media including audio and video, video discs, computer assisted learning and home experiment kits, but even today when multimedia is widely available print is still probably the most common medium.

The other element, the support services, operate while the course is in progress and involve human interaction, though often via some technical medium. Acàdemic support services concern interactions that facilitate the learning process and may include face-to-face tutorials, telephone tutorials, video links, outreach visits, on-campus study schools, as well as written correspondence, possibly through assignments. Other types of support services associated with learning at a distance are administrative support, for example, enrollment advice and counseling.

In a discussion of distance education definitions, Keegan (1986, p. 49) lists the main elements of a definition as:

- the quasi-permanent separation of teacher and learner throughout the length of the learning process; this distinguishes it from conventional face-to-face education.

- the influence of an educational organization both in the planning and preparation of learning materials and in the provision of student support services; this distinguishes it from private study and teach-yourself programs.

- the use of technical media; print, audio, video or computer, to unite teacher and learner and carry the content of the course.

- the provision of two-way communication so that the student may benefit from or even initiate dialogue; this distinguishes it from other uses of technology in education.

- the quasi-permanent absence of the learning group throughout the length of the learning process so that people are usually taught as individuals and not in groups, with the possibility of occasional meetings for both didactic and socialization purposes.

This definition of distance education has been widely quoted, but it is not universally accepted. Several alternative definitions have been suggested, and writers have pointed out courses which do not fit neatly within the definition. Given the diversity of courses offered at a distance, someone could probably point out an exception to almost any definition. However, I cannot see that continuation of this process accomplishes a great deal.

For the purpose of this book, the above definition serves well. The element of the definition which I take to be most important is the first. The separation between teacher and learner has implications, not only for the manner of instruction, but also for the degree and nature of socialization and integration which is a prominent theme within the proposed model. The only qualm I have with the definition is with the final element. It is probably true that the majority of students do learn as individuals, but there are a significant number of courses which expect students to gather in groups at off-campus sites to receive instruction. In Chapters 14 and 15 I argue that other distance education courses might make more use of off-campus group work than is currently the case.

Open Learning

There is no universally agreed definition of distance education, but there is a greater measure of agreement than there is over the term open learning. The relationship between the two terms is itself problematic. Some use the terms open and distance learning loosely or interchangeably, so presumably equate the two. Lewis and Spencer (1986, p. 17) believe it is a misconception to equate open and distance learning. There are schemes, such as flexistudy or learning at appointment centers, which clearly fail to meet the definition of distance education yet are widely accepted as being open in nature.

Nor do Thorpe and Grugeon (1987, p. 2) believe that distance learning is open learning.

> .... the question of whether distance learning is open learning, to which we would answer that distance learning is surely a sub-set of open learning—not synonymous with it, but a particular example of one type. 'Open learning' is an umbrella term which refers to a whole series of varied educational initiatives and provision.

Others such as Manwaring (1986, p. 3) also regard distance education as a subset of open learning. Fay (1988, p. 3) puts it less kindly, describing open learning as "a rag-bag or portmanteau term."

It should already be clear that there is no succinct, universally agreed definition of open learning. The closest approximation to a definition consists of a listing of aspects of openness against which courses or programs can be assessed. The version which seems to be quoted or cited most often is by Lewis and Spencer (1986). They proposed that courses be assessed on a spectrum from closed to open for each of a number of facets including:

- open entry
- study anywhere
- start any time
- tutors on demand
- attendance at any time
- flexible sequence
- negotiated objectives and content
- negotiated learning method
- negotiated assessment.

The above list obviously shows the open end of the spectrum. It lists qualities which are generally seen as desirable. The very term "open" is itself clearly a desirable one and certainly preferable to closed.

The positive connotations of the term open have created problems with definitions as courses have been labeled open even if they satisfy very few of the above criteria. Rumble (1989) proposed that it was a misuse of language to apply the epithet open as widely as it has been. He was particularly scathing about courses designed by specific companies, offered only to their own employees at fixed times. Yet these courses were cited as case-studies in a book on open learning.

There are also difficulties with Lewis and Spencer's (1986) definition if the term open learning is applied to credit courses taught at a distance. There has been a recent tendency for the descriptor open learning to be used more widely, partly out of fashion and partly because it has more positive connotations. Courses described as off-campus or external are perceived, in some quarters, as inferior to traditional full-time on-campus courses. University credit courses taught by distance education often, though, satisfy few of the above aspects of openness. The students may have reasonable choice as to where and when they study, and some, but certainly not all, courses do have open entry policies for mature students. Beyond that, however, there is often limited flexibility. Distance education courses for formal credit are often particularly constrained with respect to aspects of teaching such as sequence, assessment and choice of modules, content and objectives.

Kember and Murphy (1990) pointed out that many distance education courses which described themselves as open, in fact have less aspects of openness than a typical progressive primary school classroom. Many such classrooms would have to be classified as open on the last four of the elements of openness listed above. Instinctively, however, it does not seem right to include the primary school classroom under the open learning umbrella. Certainly the teachers did not base their teaching methods on any of the models or theories of open learning. Rather the teaching method would have been derived from educational theories which might be labeled student-centered learning.

These definition problems appear to have arisen because Lewis and Spencer's table (1986) subsumes in open learning elements of student-centered learning. Open learning has largely resulted from social and political pressures, so has concentrated on removing participation barriers. Student-centered learning resulted from educational models or philosophies, so has striven to increase freedom and student initiative within classrooms.

The reason we intuitively reject the primary classroom from the open learning category is almost certainly because we visualize open learning as being for adults. If this is the case then it can help with defining open learning if it explicitly incorporates dimensions of adult learning theory. The elements of openness can be arranged in two dimensions. One would include the political and social access criteria which are towards the top of the above list. The other dimension would incorporate facets of adult learning theory which are intimately related to the student-centered learning qualities included by Lewis and Spencer.

Before showing this two dimensional model or definition it is first necessary to refer briefly to adult learning theory. This brings in another element in the book title, namely courses for adult learners.

Adult Learning

The Centre for Educational Research and Innovation (CERI) defines an adult student as one aged 25 or over on entry to a course (1987, p. 29). It is not easy to quarrel with this definition, except perhaps by seeking to add or subtract a year or two.

Under this definition an ever growing number of students in colleges and universities are adults. The need for certification and for education to be viewed as a continuing or lifelong need have brought an increasing number of adults into universities. Some attend for the first time, others return for upgrading or additional expertise. The majority of these adult students are part-time due to other commitments but some do enroll full-time.

The very existence of a discipline called adult education implies that adult educators, at least, believe that there are differences between the learning needs and abilities of adult students and younger students. Such a distinction becomes important since most of the literature on learning and teaching is oriented towards and derived from research on younger students. Yet, the needs and orientation of adult learners do not always coincide with those of their younger counterparts.

Knowles (1970; 1984) has conveniently encapsulated the distinction between adult and adolescent education in the contrast between "andragogy" and "pedagogy" respectively. Knowles (1990, pp. 54-63) distinguishes pedagogy from andragogy by six assumptions for each. These assumptions are summarized in Table 1-1.

The table certainly does not encompass the entire wisdom on the education of adults but does provide a conveniently succinct starting point for a discussion of the characteristics of suitable teaching for adult students. Brookfield (1986, p. 91) has described andragogy as the "single most popular idea in the education and training of adults." There have been criticisms of andragogy (e.g., Day & Baskett, 1982; Hartree, 1984; Pratt, 1984). For the purposes of this book, though, andragogy needs to be accepted only at the level interpreted by McKenzie (1977) as a philosophical construct used to prescribe good practice in the teaching of adults.

Table 1-1: Pedagogy Compared to Andragogy

	PEDAGOGY	ANDRAGOGY
1. The need to know	The teacher defines the course content.	Adults expect to understand the relevance of a course to their needs.
2. The learner's self-concept	Student seen as dependent, needing direction from teacher.	Adult is a mature, responsible person capable of self-direction.
3. The role of experience	Any experiences of the students are not seen as valuable.	The experience of adults is a rich and important learning resource.
4. Readiness to learn	The teacher decides what will be learned and when.	Allows the learner to decide what is to be learned and when.
5. Orientation to learning	Learning is seen as acquiring subject-matter content.	Learning is seen as necessary for performing tasks or solving problems in daily life.
6. Motivation	External motivations are assumed.	Intrinsic motivation has primacy over extrinsic.

It might also be noted that Knowles defines pedagogy very narrowly. It is often used to refer to the science of teaching in a very general sense. Knowles restricts its applicability to the teaching of adolescents. Even then it assumes a highly teacher-centered model of adolescent teaching which does not do justice to the instances of innovative student-centered teaching which can be readily observed in schools. Nevertheless, the continuum between pedagogy and andragogy does provide a useful yardstick against which curriculum assumptions and teaching practices can be gauged. In doing so, though, it is important to be aware of the narrow definition Knowles has assigned to the pedagogy end of the continuum.

Open Learning for Adults

The elements of andragogy are closely related to the aspects of the definition of open learning which were derived from student-centered learning. This is hardly surprising given that both open and adult learning theorists would readily admit to the influence of prominent figures in the student-centered learning literature such as Dewey (1929) and Rogers (1969).

The criteria for openness given by Lewis and Spencer (1986) seem to have been derived in an arbitrary fashion. When the intention is to concentrate upon courses for adults it therefore seems reasonable to substitute the six assumptions of andragogy for the criteria related to student-centered learning. The assumptions of andragogy are based upon a synthesis of the extensive literature on adult learning (Knowles 1970; 1984) and since their formulation have been the subject of considerable discussion (e.g., Brookfield, 1986).

A synthesis of adult and open learning can be obtained by relating the assumptions of andragogy to the criteria for open learning concerned with the removal of participation barriers. The retained elements of open learning would then be a more accurate reflection of its historical origins. These resulted largely from social and political pressures for greater access to educational opportunities for adult students.

The model by Lewis and Spencer (1986) is one dimensional, along an open to closed axis. To recognize the distinct but related nature of the elements of andragogy, I propose a two dimensional model shown in Figure 1-1. One axis of the model retains the open to closed continuum, but restricts the course elements assessed to those concerned with participation barriers. The other axis ranges from pedagogy to andragogy. Treating pedagogy and andragogy as a continuum seems to be consistent with more recent interpretations by Knowles (1990) of the two teaching assumptions. The axis, therefore, provides a way of appraising the nature of the teaching and learning in open learning courses which does have a sound theoretical basis.

Figure 1-1: Adult / Open Learning Courses

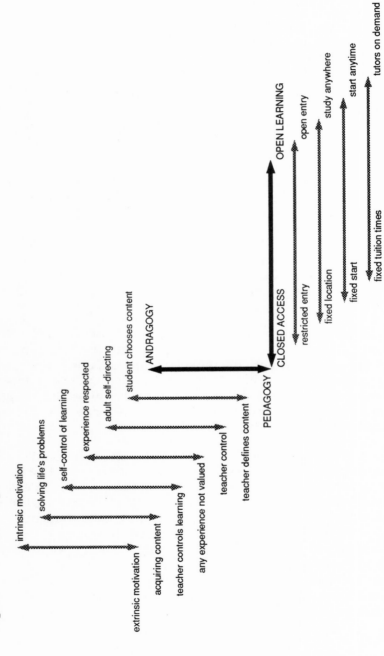

This adult/open learning diagram essentially provides a model for open learning courses for adults. It might then be treated as an ideal towards which open learning courses might aspire. It is unrealistic, and in some cases undesirable, to expect all open learning courses to be at the open and andragogy ends of the continua.

Individual courses can be assessed against the dimensions of openness and against the assumptions of andragogy. Obviously this is an approximate and in some cases highly subjective procedure. Following through this process should help resolve the anomalous cases of courses which claim to be open in their title or prospectus but have significant participation barriers. Separating the participation and adult learning qualities into discrete axes resolves anomalies arising from the inclusion of student-centered learning attributes in the criteria of openness.

For the purposes of this book, the open/adult learning model provides a descriptor and a definition of the type of course with which the book is concerned. It also suggests qualities towards which such courses might aspire.

Part-time Students

A characteristic shared by the large majority of adult learners is that they are part-time students. Society normally anticipates that schooling is a full-time occupation. Those who proceed straight from school to college or university most often do so as full-time students. Yet, adults are normally expected to combine their education with existing commitments to their work and families.

One obvious distinction between these two situations is the time available for study. As the term implies, the full-time student can devote a normal working day, and more, to study. The adult student usually has what is left after the working day plus time available at weekends. The same program of study will inevitably take the adult student considerably longer than it would take by full-time study. A degree which would take three years of full-time study might normally be expected to extend to six or seven years of part-time study. Such durations pose considerable problems in themselves.

A further distinction lies in the number of conflicting demands upon the two types of student. Full-time students have typically left school recently and perhaps live on-campus. Their social world often centers around campus life. They probably have limited responsibilities, commitments or conflicts beyond their role as a student.

The adult part-time student, however, is often in full-time employment. This not only takes time away from study but can raise conflicting demands. Many adult students have families who compete for time and attention with the study demands. The social circle of the adult student often has no overlap with the student cohort and this too can create tensions.

These distinctions between full-time and part-time students are seen as fundamental to an understanding of the respective influences upon the academic progress of the two types of student. The status of adults in open learning courses as part-time students is a vital factor in determining their success or otherwise. The part-time status of most adult students is, therefore, integral to the development of the model proposed in this book.

Summary

From the definitions given, and probably from experience too, the reader will no-doubt realize that the terms distance education and open learning can cover a diverse range of courses. The terms continue to be used loosely and for the purposes of this book that is not a problem. My intention is for the model developed in the book to apply to as wide a range of courses as possible. I will therefore interchange between the terms distance and open learning, using whichever seems more appropriate at the time.

In general, I will assume that students spend the majority of their study time away from the main campus of their college, so they are distance learners. I will also assume some element of openness about courses, and where important I will be specific as to which element of openness is being considered.

I will consistently consider adult part-time students. The determining factor in this instance is whether the students have significant commitments to work, family and social lives in addition to their role as a part-time student. The assimilation of the student role into the pattern of existing and on-going commitments is a major issue within the book. As this is a vital concern for all part-time adult students, much of the contents of the book are likely to be relevant to all courses for adults whether at a distance or not.

Chapter 2

Student Progress and Drop-out

Synopsis

Drop-out from courses has long been regarded as a problem, as it is seen as implying a wastage of resources and can create grave disappointment for the students who do not complete courses. Research in this area has, therefore, often looked for ways in which the drop-out rates might be ameliorated. From a more positive and wider perspective, research into factors affecting student progress in courses can provide policy guidelines for establishing and operating courses. There is currently very little in the way of empirically based work to help choose between the wide variety of formats that can be, and are used for open learning courses.

Drop-out is particularly pertinent for open learning courses and other courses offered to adult students because of the high rates of drop-out relative to full-time courses. The magnitude of this difference can be confused unless care is taken over definition. There is a need to recognize different categories of non-completers such as:

- non-starters

- informal withdrawals who stopped working on the course

- formal withdrawals who completed an official withdrawal procedure

- academic failures

- non-continuers who may never have intended to complete a full program of academic study.

Rationale

Whether or not students complete a degree for which they have
enrolled is a cause for interest or concern to several parties.
Students can derive considerable psychological and material
benefits from completing an academic course. On the other hand
those who do not complete their program can feel disappointed,
if not distraught. Students failing to proceed with courses usually
means a loss of revenue for universities and colleges. Some
correspondence colleges, though, insist on payment in advance to
restrict their financial losses and possibly even benefit if they do
not have to teach students full courses. Attrition rates are a
performance indicator used to assess the success of educational
institutions. Governments normally see attrition from courses as
implying an inefficient use of resources, and high drop-out rates
make them suspicious about the quality of an institution. Faculty
feel disappointed if competent students drop-out for non-
academic reasons, though there are some who seem to feel that a
significant failure rate is an indicator of the high standard of their
course!

Given this widespread concern for the effects of student
persistence, it is hardly surprising that it has been the topic for
innumerable research studies encompassing all major educational
sectors. Chapters 3 and 4 review the literature more pertinent to
this book.

Drop-out rates for distance education and open learning courses
are usually higher than those for comparable courses for full-time
students. It is not surprising, therefore, that drop-out has been a
major area for research. Garrison (1987) believes that no other
area has received more attention. Rekkedal (1985) asserted that it
was the problem which has been given the highest priority
among researchers.

The earlier persistence research in distance education often
seemed to be seeking a simple remedy to reduce attrition to levels
closer to those of full-time courses. When a simple solution was
not found, this line of research seemed to become less fashionable
and some seemed to accept relatively high drop-out levels as
inevitable.

The justification for pursuing this line of research does not rest
entirely with the issue of reducing attrition. There is also the more
positive aspect of determining factors which contribute to the

success of students in adult and open learning courses. The aim, in essence, is to build a model which will indicate the factors which are most important in contributing to students completing a course and satisfying their academic goals.

Such a model clearly has intrinsic interest. It should also have policy implications by suggesting ways to arrange courses so as to maximize the chances of students successfully completing them. The plethora of formats for open learning and distance education courses substantiate the need for a coherent theory. Clearly some of the diversity in the way courses are arranged and offered is a response to local conditions and constraints. However, there are also numerous examples of courses in similar regions teaching closely aligned areas of content, but with markedly different instructional systems, support services and administrative arrangements. In the absence of sound theory, and with limited evidence from comparative program evaluation, this diversity is almost inevitable. At present there is little in the way of established theory on which to base a valid choice.

Magnitude of Drop-out

Few would question the assertion that drop-out from distance education and open learning courses is an issue which has been of wide interest and concern. Establishing the magnitude of the problem, or citing drop-out rates, is not an easy process, though.

Firstly, institutions are usually extremely coy about publicizing their drop-out rates, as Connors (1980) and Shale (1982) have also observed. Even where data is available it may be of limited value, particularly for comparison purposes, because of the variety of ways in which students can fail to complete courses and the alternative definitions and measuring procedures used by institutions. The problems of definition and measurement will be dealt with in the next section.

From the figures which are available it can easily be seen that attrition is considerable. Glatter and Wedell (1971) reviewed correspondence courses and concluded that drop-out was much higher than in full-time courses and could reach 70%. I suspect that even this figure was largely based on the better courses and more proficient institutions, which were willing to release figures.

Shale (1982) reports course completion rates for Athabasca University of 28.8%, though these rose to 58.2% if non-starters were excluded. Woodley (1987) maintains that just over fifty percent of students who complete the registration process at the Open University of the United Kingdom will eventually obtain a degree. It is pertinent to point out, though that, of the 1982 intake, 28% of provisionally registered students did not complete the final registration process.

In the distance education university in Venezuela the drop-out rate was 79% (Rumble, 1982a, p. 199). At the Sukhothai Thammathirat Open University of Thailand, 62% of students were no longer enrolled after two years (Wichit Srisa-An, 1984, p. 334). In Costa Rica's open university, 76% had dropped out by the end of their fifth semester (Rumble, 1982b, p. 82). In Pakistan's distance teaching university some courses reported drop-out rates as high as 99.5% as early as the first semester (Fleming, 1982, p. 143). This brief review is sufficient to show that open learning institutions, wherever in the world they are, should not be surprised if they lose half or more of their enrolling students.

These overall figures vary appreciably from institution to institution and there would also be marked variations within institutions. Inter-institutional comparison is difficult because of different ways of calculating attrition, a problem which is discussed in the next section. Even from the figures above, it can be seen that excluding non-starters can make a large difference to completion rates.

Within institutions it is normal to find considerable variation in attrition by degree and even more by the subjects or courses which make up a degree (e.g., Shale, 1982). Not unexpectedly these variations tend to relate to the nature of the courses. Graduate programs tend to have lower attrition rates than first degrees. Longer programs usually have lower competition rates than short ones. Shale (1982) gives completion figures (excluding non-starters) of 68.6% and 52.8% for 3-credit and 6-credit courses respectively, for Athabasca University.

Within a course, attrition is usually higher, and often much higher, in the early stages than towards the end. The fact that some institutions quote attrition figures excluding non-starters which are appreciably lower than those for all enrolled students, is one indicator of the magnitude of initial drop out. Time series studies by Kember (1981) and McIntosh, Woodley and Morrison

(1980) show steeper slopes on attrition or survival graphs in the initial stages.

Not surprisingly, attrition rates for open learning and distance education courses are normally higher than those for full-time education. Once again comparison is not straightforward because of the difference in measuring procedures and because full-time courses, too, show considerable variation in attrition rates. Comparisons can be made in Australian institutions which offer the same course in different modes. Two studies by Smith (1976; 1979) showed that full-time students were less likely to withdraw than part-time students, who in turn were less likely to withdraw than correspondence students.

Defining Attrition

As Tinto has pointed out (1975, p. 89) past research on drop-outs from higher education has often given inadequate attention to definition by failing to distinguish either permanent drop-outs from temporary withdrawals, or drop-out because of academic failure and voluntary withdrawal. For distance education clear definition is of special importance because of the variety of procedures among institutions for registration and recording student progress or withdrawal.

It is common for students to enroll or register for open learning courses but then to submit no assignments at all. Informal withdrawals are often concentrated right at the start of a course. There can be significant numbers of students who are best described as non-starters. They complete the formal enrollment procedures and receive their initial study materials, but make no further contact with the institution.

Because of these early withdrawals and non-starters, the starting point of a course also needs careful definition. Many institutions count course enrollment a few weeks after the start of a course. This procedure allows enrollments to settle down. It gives the student record database a chance to cope with late enrollments, transfers, and the tribulations of the start of a semester or academic year. The precise timing of the effective enrollment date can, though, markedly affect drop-out rates if initial withdrawals are high. Even a week or two either way can make appreciable differences to attrition statistics.

As a result of early drop-out problems, some institutions have a trial period at the beginning of a course of study. An example is the Open University of the United Kingdom, where students who accept the offer of a place pay a provisional registration fee. The provisional registration period lasts for three months of the first year of study and at the end of this period the student has to decide whether to pay the full registration fee (McIntosh, Woodley & Morrison, 1980, p. 48).

A growing number of institutions also offer short introductory or orientation courses (e.g., Bowser & Race, 1991), designed mainly for the mature age entrant, to raise awareness of the problems faced and the study techniques needed for distance education courses. So when discussing attrition it should be made clear whether the enrollment is counted before or after such trial periods and introductory courses.

There are then a variety of ways that a registered student can fail to complete and pass a course. There are students who formally withdraw from a course, but there are also students who cease sending in assignments without formally withdrawing. The latter group of students are normally regarded as failing a course in formal recording procedures. A student may also complete all assignments but not reach the required standard in either continuous or final assessment and thus fail on academic grounds. If possible these three categories of withdrawal, informal withdrawal and academic failure should be distinguished, though recording procedures often make this difficult.

A complication arises when students accumulate credits towards a degree or diploma and are permitted to take time off between the individual credits. The Open University of the United Kingdom, for example, allows students to take as many years as they like to obtain a degree so they have to present their graduation rates as cumulative proportions graduating over a period of at least eight years (McIntosh, Woodley & Morrison, 1980, p. 49). After this time the graph has begun to level out as few students persist to complete a degree after such lengthy periods; though presumably the Open University is unable to finally remove non-completers from its records till death us do part.

Students can also discontinue their study in one institution and transfer to another to complete their course. Normally the latter institution grants credit for the proportion of the course completed in the first institution. The initial institution may be quite unaware that students have enrolled elsewhere so transferring students are classified with other withdrawing or discontinuing students. Students starting with credit create problems for research designs as they can behave quite differently to other students starting at the same time with no prior credit.

One defense against high drop-out rates cited by open learning universities is that some students enroll without intending to complete a program. They take the modules or subjects they feel necessary for their career needs and then stop studying. Andragogy (Knowles, 1970; 1984) recognizes the ability of adult students to define their own learning needs. Universities and colleges, though, still concentrate, in the main, on offering complete degree programs. Most have been slow to adapt to the growing continuing education needs resulting from the pace of change in technology and information. Graduates increasingly need to upgrade their knowledge and skills but do not necessarily need to complete a whole degree program for these purposes.

It would be useful to have studies which track cohorts of students enrolling for open learning courses on a semester by semester basis. At each point the proportion of students which fit into the various categories below should be recorded:

- those who commence with prior credit
- non-starters
- informal withdrawals who stopped working on the course
- formal withdrawals who completed an official withdrawal procedure
- academic failure
- those who pass but do not enroll for a subsequent course
- those who pass and enroll for a subsequent course
- those who transfer to other programs.

The paths for student progress is visualized in Figure 2-1. This diagram shows alternative paths into, out of and through programs towards graduation. The diagram assumes a straightforward linear progression of course modules or units. Many programs allow students to take more than one unit per semester and to choose from a range of optional modules.

Figure 2-1: Potential Paths into and out of Courses

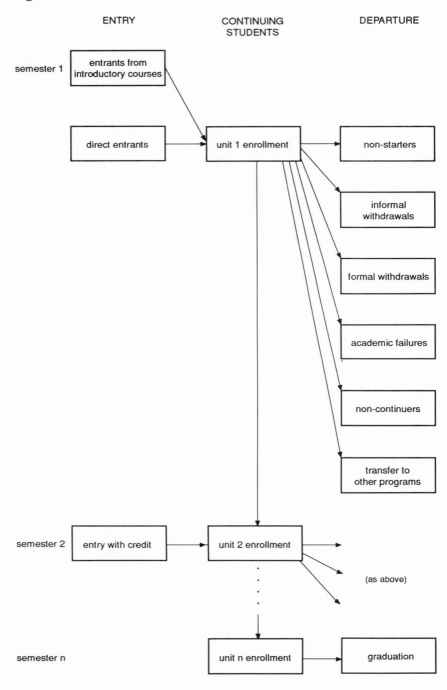

Diagrams like those in Figure 2-1 would obviously be more useful if they indicated the percentages of students taking each of the potential paths. To allow for choice between modules they could be computed by years since enrollment point. Data for some of the paths, particularly those for transferring students and unofficial withdrawals, are difficult to obtain from many institutions' student record systems. In many instances students on these paths will be shown in other categories. Nevertheless, even a diagram without several potential paths will contain valuable information. It would enable institutions to see what happens to their students, to ascertain areas of greatest attrition and to better predict continuing enrollment patterns. It would also help researchers provide better definitions of what is meant by drop-out and its various synonyms.

Until more progress is made towards agreement on common definition of terms and analysis of data, each institution needs to make clear how any figures were calculated. In papers, researchers must show their formulae for determining enrollment and withdrawal statistics and specify the points in time at which measurements were made.

In the long run it is possible that there will be a trend towards greater commonality in definitions and recording procedures. Governments are showing increasing interest in the use of performance indicators, such as completion rates, in an effort to make educational institutions more accountable. Clearly performance indicators are of little value unless measured consistently. Part of the process of introducing them is, therefore, to decide on definitions, measuring procedures and reporting formats.

Conclusion

Attrition has always been a major concern for distance education courses. While it may be difficult to give precise figures there is no doubt that significant proportions of students drop-out from most open learning courses. Not surprisingly, drop-out rates tend to be higher than those for full-time on-campus courses.

Simple solutions have not been found, and almost certainly never will be. If the drop-out process is to be explained it will be in terms of a model which incorporates the wide variety of possible factors which might induce students to discontinue a course. It should also allow for the interaction of these factors.

The search for a more complex model of this type has the important benefit of additionally contributing to an understanding of more positive outcomes. Such a model should also point towards ways to assist students to complete courses and to perform well academically. As such any model could provide valuable guidance in the formulation of distance education programs.

Beyond these observations it is difficult to make a succinct summary of the points in this chapter because there is little if any agreement on definitions and wide diversity in practice on calculating any figures which are reported. The most useful summary is Figure 2-1 which shows the variety of possible paths into and out of programs. Until institutions start to recognize these potential routes for students when presenting data the figures will have limited meaning. Comparable performance data will only emerge when common definitions are agreed which take into account the alternative outcomes.

Chapter 3

Theories of Persistence

Synopsis

More recent research has regarded student persistence as a multi-variate problem involving complex interactions over the period of the course. Along these lines models have been developed by Spady, Tinto, Bean and others. The work of Tinto has been particularly influential. Tinto's (1975) model drew upon Durkheim's (1961) theory of suicide to suggest that students were most likely to drop-out if they were insufficiently integrated with the fabric of college society. Two types of integration were considered, namely moral or value integration and collective affiliation. A subsequent development of the model by Tinto (1987) drew upon Van Gannep's (1960) concept of the "rites of passage" to suggest that successful students are most likely to achieve integration through moving from membership in their previous social community to college society.

The concept of integration developed by Tinto has been operationalized and tested by a number of researchers. The success of the model is evidenced by its influence on much of the current persistence research.

Introduction

When I started research into the area of student progress and drop-out there was no adequate conceptual model applicable to distance education courses. In the next chapter I argue that the model developed in this book is the first comprehensive model of student progress for open learning courses for adults to be extensively tested.

In the wider field of more conventional education, there has been considerably more extensive research and greater progress in formulating conceptual models of the drop-out process. In this chapter, I will present a selective review of the voluminous literature on persistence and drop-out from mainstream education courses. I will concentrate on work which is relevant to the conceptual model developed in this book. In particular I will examine other models which have been developed, especially those which were influential and inspirational to this work. I will also highlight work more relevant to adult students.

Early research into student persistence tended to search for entry characteristics which correlated with drop-out. This earlier persistence research has been reviewed by Cope and Hannah (1975), Pantages and Creedon (1978), Pascarella (1982) and Bean (1982).

Single variable studies served only to confirm that there is clearly not a single explanation or cure for drop-out. Even when numerous pre-enrollment characteristics were combined into multiple regression designs, the correlations normally explained only small proportions of the variance. Panos and Astin (1968), for example, collected data on 120 variables from a large sample of college students. A multiple regression of these variables produced a linear combination which explained little more than nine percent of the variance.

It is quite comforting that entry characteristics are such poor predictors of success. Students with the wrong initial data set are not pre-destined to fail, however hard they try. The faculty and the college do have a role to play in determining the success or otherwise of their students.

Even if enrollment data were a better predictor of success, such research may have had little relevance to policy decisions as selection could not be based upon many of the variables in regression equations of enrollment data for legal, political or social reasons. This was especially so in adult education since selection according to entry characteristics is often undesirable or politically unacceptable. Not surprisingly, interest in this line of research waned considerably, though, there are still people looking for single variable solutions.

Models of Persistence

As research into pre-enrollment characteristics and drop-out ran into a brick wall, there was an increasing effort devoted to the development of models of the drop-out process which related persistence to constructs and measures beyond entry characteristics.

Bean (1982) made a useful review of available models and categorized them into six types, though three of the categories contain just one model in his review. Most of the models cited by Bean related to conventional higher education. Before starting work on a model applicable to open learning courses for adults, though, it was pertinent to examine these models to derive an appropriate framework from what had been learnt in other educational arenas.

The first category contained atheoretical descriptive studies that really do not deserve to be called models at all. The second framework contained studies which concentrated on pre-matriculation characteristics. Again it is questionable whether the term "model" is appropriate. The limitations of this type of work have been discussed in the previous section.

The third type of model was the person-role fit model, which focused on the relationship between individual characteristics and the requirements of the student's role at a particular institution. The only example cited by Bean was that of Rootman (1972). Thompson's (1984) proposed model for distance education students could also be included in this category. He suggested that drop-out was related to the cognitive style of field dependence.

A series of studies by Boshier on New Zealand adult education students, also built towards a model in this category. Boshier (1971) used Houle's typology of motivational orientation to develop a model of adult education participation in which students are classified as "being" or "deficiency" motivated. A later Boshier (1972) study developed a scale based on Carl Rogers' self-concept theory. This scale was subsequently used (Boshier, 1973) in a congruence model based on self theory to account for drop-out and participation.

Bean located the Fishbein and Ajzen model (1975) in a category that was labeled "the importance of intentions in influencing behavior." The model postulated a sequence, with a feedback loop, of belief about the consequences of a behavior, the attitude toward the behavior, the intention to perform the behavior, and finally the behavior itself. Although it may be possible to find good correlations between attitude, intention, and behavior, such findings suggest little about the consequences of possible interventions designed to reduce drop-out.

A group of three models were categorized as longitudinal-process models. Each of the models treated attrition as a longitudinal process in which background characteristics influence the way in which the student interacts with the college environment, which in turn influences educational and attitudinal outcomes, which eventually culminates in a decision on drop-out. Two of the models related the drop-out process to Durkheim's (1961) model of suicide. Durkheim postulated that suicide was more likely to occur with individuals who were insufficiently integrated into the fabric of society. In the models, suicide is equated to dropping-out, and society is equated with the learning institution. The three models were generally more complex than those previously discussed but do present an easily visualized picture of the processes and events in the path from enrollment to drop-out or completion.

The three models in this category were closely related. The first model to be based upon Durkheim's work was by Spady (1970; 1971). The Tinto (1975) model was more linear than Spady's but contained similar elements. The third longitudinal model (Pascarella, 1980) was based on the previous two but emphasized student-faculty informal contacts.

A further model not reviewed by Bean (1982) could perhaps best be placed in this category. It is a model of nontraditional undergraduate student attrition (Bean & Metzner, 1985). The model indicates that drop-out decisions will be based primarily on four sets of variables, background and defining, academic, environmental, and social integration. The model also takes cognizance of academic and psychological outcomes and intent to leave. Distance education is presumably nontraditional, but there is a difference between distance education students and the definition of nontraditional students chosen by Bean and Metzner (1985, p. 488). They state that "a nontraditional student usually does not live in a college residence and therefore must commute to classes." Their nontraditional students therefore receive instruction via face-to-face classes, whereas the primary vehicle of content and instruction for distance education students is the package of study materials or mediated lessons. Because the drop-out models in this category focus on the quantity and quality of student-student and student-faculty interactions, this difference is very significant.

The final category contains an industrial model of student attrition based on a study of nurse turnover by Price and Mueller (1981). The adapted model by Bean (1983) contained ten variables which reflected the students' interaction with the organization and two variables external to the organization. Bean (1982) also presents a synthetic model developed from his review.

Tinto's Model

In choosing a model to influence similar work in a different study mode, those in the longitudinal-process category had the greatest appeal. A longitudinal model is attractive in that it has provision for interpreting the effect on the student of the course and support services provided by the institution and the degree to which study is compatible with the student's lifestyle. It recognizes the potential impact of interventions by the institution and events in the student's life rather than merely relating the drop-out phenomenon to a set of apparently predestined variables.

Of the models in the category, that by Tinto (1975) was the most widely respected. According to Bean (1982), the Tinto model was both the most widely cited and the most widely tested empirically. More recent writers have noted that Tinto's model continues in a pre-eminent position. Christie and Dinham (1991, p. 412) believe that it is "one of the most widely accepted views of institutional departure." Cabrera, Castañeda, Nora and Hengstler (1992, p. 144) note that the model "has served as the conceptual framework for numerous studies." Brower (1992, p. 442) asserts that the Tinto model is "the one most often used."

It has not only been used to interpret attrition studies in face-to-face teaching but has been cited in studies related to distance education. Malley, Brown and Williams (1976), Smith (1979), Kember (1981), Thompson (1984), Sweet (1986), and Taylor *et al.* (1986) have all drawn upon constructs within the model to interpret research findings. It is important that researchers find a model to be of value in interpreting their findings. Therefore the Tinto model would appear to be the best starting point for a model of persistence applicable to open learning and distance education courses.

The model developed in this book draws heavily upon constructs developed by Tinto in his original model of persistence (1975) and in his subsequent theoretical development of the work (1987). It is, therefore, pertinent to examine in greater detail both the model itself and two constructs on which Tinto based his development of the model. These two constructs, which are examined in turn, are Van Gannep's (1960) work on "rites of passage" and Durkheim's (1961) theory of suicide. Tinto drew analogies between both of these sociological models and the influences on student drop-out.

Rites of Passage

Van Gannep (1960) envisaged an individual's life as a series of passages marked by changes in group membership or the individual's status. He believed that rituals and ceremonies eased the dislocation and disruption which accompanies these changes. The function of the ceremonies was both to announce the new status of the novitiate and also to provide a mechanism to introduce the new group and assist the newcomers to become established within it.

Van Gannep asserted that change from one status or group to another was a three-phase process, with discrete stages of separation, transition and incorporation. Separation implies a decrease in interactions with membership of the group that the individual is leaving. It can be accompanied by a ceremony indicating that membership of that group is no longer necessary to the leaver. Transition sees the start of interaction with the new group and learning about their norms and behaviors. Van Gannep observed that training, isolation or ordeals were rites which could accompany the transition phase. Incorporation means becoming accepted as a member of the new group and performing functions implied by membership. It can be marked by a ceremony announcing that the new group has been joined and certifying the obligations and privileges that entails.

Tinto (1987) saw a parallel between Van Gannep's stages in rites of passage and the movement of students from the high school community to college or university. Tinto saw this transition as being generally similar to the passage of individuals between human communities. He, further, saw that the students' ability to overcome the problems of adjustment and become incorporated into the new college community would have a major influence on whether they persisted as a member of college society.

The first phase of changing status from high school graduate to college student consists of separation from high school friends and the local community. Students who physically move to live on a college campus need to undergo a social and emotional transplantation too. Those unable to put aside their ties to their local community may be unable to make the transition to become members of college society.

Tinto notes that those who attend a local, non-residential college face less of a dislocation as they do not have to re-locate away from their existing social and family relationships. However, because these students do not disentangle themselves from their existing web of relationships, any ties they establish with the new college community are likely to be weaker. As a result they may find it easier to cope with the initial move to higher education but subsequently find that they have less entrenched relationships with their new environment than those who undergo a more intrusive break with their social relationships.

The second transition phase requires students to adapt to the conventions of college life and establish themselves within the social and intellectual community of the college. The ease with which students cope with this transition depends on how closely their academic conception and social circle match those of the college which they are entering. Clearly those with a conception of academic study which does not match the expectations of academia will find this transition difficult (Perry, 1970; 1988). Similarly those who come from a different social background to the majority of their college community are likely to find difficulties with the transition process. The greater the difference between the norms of college behavior and that of the student's home community, the more difficult the transition process is likely to be. The obvious implication of this statement is that the greatest difficulties are likely to be faced by those from minority groups, overseas students, mature entrants or those from small rural or isolated communities.

The final phase is that of incorporation into the social and intellectual fabric of college or university society. Few universities and colleges arrange much which resembles ceremony or ritual to mark this passage. In the main it is left to less formal student-student and faculty-student contacts to provide an integrative mechanism. If the process is successful the newcomer will eventually feel that he or she has become an established member of the college community.

Christie and Dinham (1991) interviewed 25 students at a large US university to examine their passage into the university community. They concluded that Tinto's interpretation of Van Gannep's work provided a useful framework for interpreting their data. They found evidence that students who maintained contacts with high school friends made less progress towards integrating into the university community. Living on campus and participating in extra-curricular activities were mechanisms for incorporation. Christie and Dinham (1991, p. 433) believed that their findings indicated that external commitments are a stronger influence on persistence than might be indicated by Tinto's model.

Tierney (1992) criticized Tinto's interpretation of Van Gannep's work following an anthropological analysis. He asserted that traditionally all initiates survive rites of passage—there are no drop-outs. He also pointed out that rituals were part of the development of individuals through stages within a culture. They were not developed to accompany transitions between one culture and another as might happen when an individual from a minority group enters a university.

Durkheim's Theory of Suicide

To examine the issues of whether and how students become integrated into college society, Tinto turned to the work of Durkheim (1961) on suicide. Durkheim classified suicide into four types: altruistic, anomic, fatalistic and egotistical. The first three of these concern suicide from societies of particular types or at times when specific conditions impinge.

Egotistical suicide is the form which is most relevant to student persistence because it is symptomatic of individuals who become isolated from society's communities because of an inability to integrate and establish membership. Durkheim noted that suicide could occur if two forms of integration were lacking. The first was social integration, which occurred through interaction with other members of society and led to the formation of personal affiliations. The second was value or intellectual integration, which resulted when there was insufficient commonality in values and beliefs with those of the relevant community.

Durkheim argued that if either form of integration were lacking, there was some press towards suicide, as individuals would become either social isolates or intellectual deviants. Egotistical suicide is normally accompanied by the lack of both social and intellectual integration. The concurrence of both conditions precludes the intellectual deviant from social integration in a deviant community or the social isolate from concurring with society's values expressed via the media.

The likelihood of an individual committing egotistical suicide depends upon that individual's ability to establish social and intellectual integration. The overall rate of egotistical suicide within a particular society depends on the nature of that society and upon the presence of integrative mechanisms to enable individuals to become established as members of intellectual and social communities.

Spady (1971) and subsequently Tinto (1975) saw an analogy between Durkheim's theory of suicide and drop-out from college society. They postulated that drop-out was more likely to occur among students who were unable to establish membership of the college's social community or who differed from the prevailing values and intellectual norms of the college. Institutions which were not able to provide mechanisms by which students can achieve these forms of integration are likely to be those with high drop-out rates.

Tinto's Model of Student Integration

The model which Tinto synthesized from previous attrition research and more particularly from the work of Durkheim is shown in Figure 3-1. The first part of the model contains entry characteristics of students, which affect succeeding elements. Next comes a component for goal and institutional commitment. The model then splits into two for academic and social systems. These influence respectively academic and social integration. The goal and institutional commitment element then re-appears before a drop-out decision is made.

Figure 3-1: Diagram of Tinto's Model

Adapted from Tinto (1975, p. 95). Reprinted with permission from the American Educational Research Association. Copyright 1975.

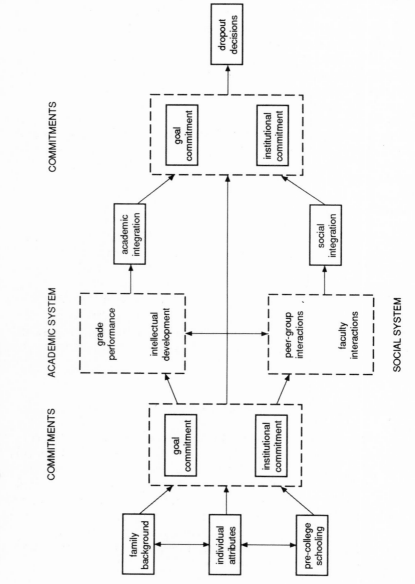

Testing of Tinto's Model

There have been a number of studies which have produced evidence to support the construct of integration in relation to drop-out and its predictive validity. Initial studies (Pascarella & Terenzini, 1977; Terenzini & Pascarella, 1977; 1978) were admitted by their authors (Terenzini, Lorang & Pascarella, 1981) to be a somewhat indirect and superficial assessment of the main constructs of the Tinto model. In a study that examined the effect of integration more directly (Pascarella & Terenzini, 1979), thirteen measures of social and academic integration were found to contribute significant statistical increases to the explanation of voluntary withdrawal from college, once the influence of student entering characteristics had been controlled for. Pascarella and Terenzini (1980) went on to develop a thirty-four-item, five factor instrument designed to measure the constructs of social and academic integration and institutional and goal commitment of the Tinto model. The study provided support for these constructs from the Tinto model because it was able to correctly classify over three-quarters of a cross-validation sample from an independent university as either persisters or withdrawals. A subsequent replication study at a large public university (Terenzini, Lorang & Pascarella, 1981) replicated almost exactly the five factor structure found in the original study and found them to be reasonably stable predictors of attrition.

Christie and Dinham (1991) have suggested that influences external to campus life play a greater role in determining persistence than might be anticipated from Tinto's model. Models developed by Bean (1982; 1983) and Bean and Metzner (1985) place greater emphasis on factors external to the organization. A comparison of the models by Cabrera, Castañeda, Nora and Hengstler (1992) concluded that factors external to the institution do play a more comprehensive and complex role than that portrayed by the Tinto model.

Conclusion

This chapter has suggested that Tinto's work is the most widely used and the best respected of currently available models of student attrition. It has been widely cited, showing that it has both predictive power and value in interpreting findings. It has been extensively tested and the results have confirmed the broad propositions of the model.

The model was developed with full-time on-campus study in mind. The social system assumed is one in which the student attends classes and socializes on a campus. The social integration component of the model deals with student-student and student-faculty interactions.

Clearly this assumed environment does not fit the situation of adult part-time students. The fit is even worse if the mode of study is distance education. Tinto (1982) did not see his original model applying to environments differing from those he had in mind when it was formulated. His work contains a caution that modifications to the model would be necessary for nontraditional forms of education.

The next chapter considers how Tinto's model can be adapted to suit the quite different learning environment of the part-time adult student enrolled in an open learning course. It starts the process of extracting from the Tinto model the theoretical bases which have proved so successful and influential and seeing how they can be adapted for this alternative mode of study. This subsequently leads to the re-forming of a complete new model in the following part of the book.

Chapter 4

Towards a Theory for Open Learning

Synopsis

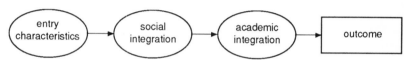

While the work of Tinto has been highly influential, there are limitations in its applicability to both open-learning and to adult education. The fact that distance education and most open learning students spend little if any time on the main college campus means that the initial interpretation of academic integration cannot be used. Measures of student-faculty interaction and absorption into campus social life clearly have little relevance.

This chapter, therefore, adapts Tinto's work to suit distance and adult education. The model developed defines academic integration to encompass all facets of the offering of the course to the student by the institution. This would include the study package and mediated lessons, any tutoring by faculty members, and any interaction between student and institution whether of an academic or administrative nature. Social integration can then refer to the degree to which the student is able to integrate the demands of part-time study with the continuing commitments of work, family and social life. These redefined social and academic integration constructs can then be seen as complex variables which impinge upon student progress once a course has started.

Distance Education Research

Before proceeding to examine the adaptation of the Tinto (1975) model, the obvious question which springs to mind is whether any existing theory or model for distance education is suitable? The chapter starts, therefore, with a review of the existing literature on drop-out, persistence and student progress in the distance education and open learning literature. The review is selective in concentrating on work which aims at building theories or models.

There has been a substantial body of research into persistence and drop-out from open learning and distance education courses. Reviews of this research have been conducted by Bååth (1984), Cookson (1990) and Garrison (1987). I see no need to provide another comprehensive review as much of the work can be categorized as either descriptive or single variable studies.

In looking at the distance education literature, I will be guided by a statement by Schuemer and Strohlein (1991). They asserted that recommendations and measures for reducing or preventing drop-out from distance education courses should be based on a causal model which has been tested empirically. I will, therefore, only discuss work which is based upon a model and critically examine any empirical test of the model.

The classification of models by Bean (1982), referred to in the previous chapter, again provides a useful framework for examining the models. Atheoretical descriptive models in the first category will not be considered.

A model which seems best placed in the second category, referring to pre-enrollment characteristics, is that of Kennedy and Powell (1976). They proposed a "descriptive model" which related the drop-out process to characteristics and circumstances. Characteristics, which are slow to change, include such variables as educational background, motivation, and personality. Circumstances, which change faster, include items such as health, finance, occupational changes and family relationships. Characteristics and circumstances are brought together in a two-dimensional model. The pressure of adverse circumstances is seen as more likely to lead to at-risk situations or drop-out for students with weak characteristics than it is for those with strong characteristics. The model is limited to providing a descriptive framework of reasons students give for dropping-out. Because it concentrates on enrollment status and circumstantial events, the model appears to make the depressing suggestion that the drop-out process is difficult to influence by the educational institution, because the characteristics of the student population can only be affected by selection of students.

Powell, Conway and Ross (1990) proposed a model containing three sets of factors; predisposing characteristics, institutional factors and life changes. However, the authors examined only the relationship between predisposing characteristics and persistence so by default their model is best placed in the same category.

There are several models in Bean's (1982) third category—the person-role fit model. Thompson's (1984) model related drop-out to the cognitive style of field dependence. Two studies by Dille and Mezack (1991) and Rayner and Schmid (1985) related drop-out to locus of control indicators and to measures of learning styles from Kolb's Learning Styles Inventory. The limitation of all work in this category is that the various cognitive styles are all measures of reasonably stable psychological characteristics. If it is found that those who display evidence of a particular style are more at-risk it is difficult to influence those students to adopt an alternative style. The alternative possibility of using cognitive style tests as a selection criterion for course entry is not one which would be seriously contemplated by many institutions.

The remaining models are all multivariate models which treat student persistence as a linear process subject to influences which operate subsequent to enrollment. Billings (1988) proposed an adaptation of Bean's (1982) model, synthesized from that of Tinto (1975) and other models. Billings' model included factors on background, organization, environment, attitude, intention and lesson submission. The model tried to reconcile the nature of study at a distance by including family and employment related variables. Brindley (1988) adapted her model from Bean and Metzner's (1985) one for adult commuter students. The variables were adapted from an examination of students' initial experiences of distance education. The models of both Billings and Brindley are perfectly plausible but as yet no attempt to operationalize or test them seems to have been reported. Without empirical testing it is difficult to have any confidence in the validity or applicability of the models. Further, the process of testing a model normally leads to refinement and development which these models have not benefited from.

Chacon (1985) started the process of developing a model by looking at bivariate relationships between completion and variables related to distance education programs. Grouping related variables into regression models then led to the formation of a path model. Two intervening variables—the difficulty of the course and the perseverance of the student—played a central role in the model. The difficulty of the course was influenced by variables such as workload, number of assignments and the quality of the instructional presentation. The limitation of Chacon's work is that it focused only on course related variables and took no account of factors outside the institution's arena. As a result it cannot be seen as a comprehensive model of the factors which impinging upon the progress of part-time students as they attempt to reconcile completing an academic course while at the same time continuing previous commitments to work and family life.

Two studies by Sweet (1986) and Bernard and Amundsen (1989) have produced models based on the work of Tinto (1975). Neither model, however, took sufficient note of Tinto's own caution (1982) that modifications need to be made to his model when applied in nontraditional settings or with nontraditional students. Sweet's (1986) variable sets appeared exactly as in the Tinto model. The variable sets were represented by a very limited number of measured variables. For example, the Tinto variable set, social integration, was measured only by the students' ratings of their exchanges with tutors. This appeared inadequate even as a measure of social influences that would arise during the time specifically allocated to study. Bernard and Amundsen (1989) include only student-faculty and student-student contacts in their social integration variable.

Neither model, therefore, takes any account of the part-time status of the students so cannot conceptualize all those social impacts on family, work, and social life that must result from a commitment to part-time off-campus study. Neither study takes any account of the rich and varied influences that the home and family situation, the demands of work and the influence of social lives have on the progress of distance education students towards course completion or withdrawal. Their models, therefore, ignore the many studies (e.g., Kember, 1989b; Kennedy & Powell, 1976; Store & Osborne, 1979; Woodley, 1987; Woodley & McIntosh, 1980) which support the contention that these environments do have a crucial impact on the progress of distance education students.

When I started work on developing a model of student progress for open learning or distance education courses, it was reasonable to claim that there was no adequate conceptual model. Models currently in existence suffer from either one of two principal deficiencies. Most have a narrow framework which excludes influences outside the immediate sphere of the institution, so have little input from or ability to explain the student perspective. The few models which have a wider focus have not been empirically tested. The distance education model which has received the widest testing is the early theoretical version (Kember, 1989a) of the model discussed in this book. Empirical tests and developments are described in Kember (1989b), Kember, Murphy, Siaw and Yuen (1991) and in Kember, Lai, Murphy, Siaw and Yuen (1992a). An independent test was conducted by Roberts, Boyton, Buete and Dawson (1991) who concluded (p. 82) that the model "provided an appropriate and workable theoretical framework for this study."

Applicability of Tinto's Model

Having ascertained that there is a need for theory development in this area, it does become worthwhile to utilize the strong theoretical foundations laid by Tinto. In doing so, though, it is important to note the caution by Tinto himself (1982) that his model needed to be modified if applied to situations differing from that of full-time on-campus study for which it was developed.

The fact that distance education and most open learning students spend little if any time on the main college campus means that the initial interpretations of academic and social integration cannot be used. Measures of student-faculty interaction and absorption into campus social life clearly have little relevance.

The part-time enrollment status of the students also necessitates modifications to Tinto's model. Work by Cabrera, Castañeda, Nora and Hengstler (1992) concluded that factors external to the institution play a more comprehensive and complex role than that portrayed by the Tinto model even for on-campus students. Clearly, external factors become increasingly important when study is a part-time activity. It becomes questionable whether the students are required or able to undergo a rite of passage when they have to maintain existing work and social commitments.

Rites of Passage

I will first consider the part of Tinto's model based upon Van Gannep's (1960) concept of rites of passage. Van Gannep saw transitions between one life stage and another as taking place through a three-phase process of separation, transition and incorporation.

The first phase has to be seen quite differently for an adult enrolling in an open learning course compared to the original interpretation of students enrolling in a college. The high school graduate can often physically leave the local community to move to a college campus. The work of Christie and Dinham (1991) suggests that those best able to extricate themselves from their former community are best placed to integrate fully with college society.

Adults, however, are not often in a position to remove themselves from their existing environment if they wish to study at college. They normally have to continue earning a living so must remain in their current employment. Many have families, which implies continuing need for support and obligations to family members. Without relocation existing social circles continue intact. Rather than separating from an existing lifestyle, the would-be student must build a new role on top of these existing commitments.

The part-time status of most adult students implies that a full separation from past associations and obligations cannot take place. Part-time students do not, therefore, face the trauma of re-locating from one community to another. However, as Tinto (1987, pp. 95-96) points out, nor do they benefit from the establishment of strong ties to a campus community. Avoiding a separation may make the initial transition easier but it makes it more difficult to build strong ties to the new society or status. Those who keep a foothold in both camps find it easier to step back into their former territory.

It is clear that the part-time adult student cannot make the full separation from past communities that is possible for high school graduates entering college. Is it possible though that a less distinct transition can be conceptualized? When considering women reentering higher education, Redding and Dowling (1992) postulate a transition in status from "non-degreed person to student to degreed person" (pp. 221-222). In their interviews they discovered evidence of rituals established by the women to formalize their new status as students.

For part-time adult students the transition may be envisaged as that from non-student to part-time student status. The transition implies building a new role on top of existing commitments. The success or otherwise of this integrative process can be conceptualized in terms of Durkheim's theory of suicide (1961) which is the other substantive theoretical element in Tinto's work.

Integration

In Durkheim's (1961) theory of suicide, egotistical suicide would not happen if individuals became integrated into the fabric of society. Two forms of integration were distinguished; collective affiliation and intellectual integration or normative congruence.

For part-time adult students, collective affiliation is achieved if a student feels some sense of belonging in a course. This sense can arise through contacts with college personnel such as tutors and even administrators. It may also come about through contacts with other students in the course.

Part-time status reduces the degree of collective affiliation which can be achieved. Firstly, there are fewer opportunities to meet with faculty and other students. Secondly, the part-time student still has a foot in another camp. The student still belongs to the social units which existed prior to enrollment. There has been no rite of passage to leave those social units so there will be less need to seek incorporation into a new environment. Any ties which do form will of necessity be weaker because of the continued existence of affiliation to other groups.

For students enrolled in distance education courses, establishing collective affiliation has an extra dimension of difficulty. Physical separation from faculty and fellow students reduces opportunities to develop relationships. Affiliation can be developed when contact is through media channels, but it is not as easy as when there is direct face-to-face contact.

Normative congruence is achieved when a student's intellectual beliefs and values are consistent with the expectations of the college and its faculty. In an academic context incongruence is most often present when a student's conceptions of knowledge and study requirements differs from academic norms and conventions.

In his model Tinto (1975) envisaged students as needing to integrate with both the academic and social environments of their college. The academic and particularly the social environments of part-time open learning students are very different from those of full-time on-campus students. These aspects of Tinto's model, therefore, need to be adapted. The tests of Tinto's model have been with instruments which contain scales measuring student-faculty and student-student contact (Pascarella & Terenzini, 1980). Many of the items in these scales would have little if any meaning for those enrolled in a distance education course.

Adaptation to Suit Open Learning

The distance education scenario is characterized by part-time, mainly mature students who study at a distance from the campus of the institution. Further, a defining characteristic of distance education (Keegan, 1986, p. 49) is "the quasi-permanent absence of the learning group throughout the length of the learning process so that people are usually taught as individuals and not in groups, with the possibility of occasional meetings for both didactic and socialization purposes."

To suit the characteristics of adult open learning students, the model proposed in this book re-defines academic integration to encompass all facets of the offering of the course to the student by the institution. These include the study package, any tutoring by faculty members, and any interaction between student and institution whether of an academic or administrative nature. Social integration can then refer to the degree to which the student is able to integrate the demands of part-time study with the continuing commitments of work, family and social life.

These redefined social and academic integration constructs can then be seen as complex variables which impinge upon student progress once a course has started. Entry characteristics will influence the degree to which both academic and social integration is possible. The extent of integration then affects the students' progress towards either successful course completion or withdrawal. Social and academic integration become intervening variables between entry characteristics and outcome measures.

Further, it is hypothesized that direct correlations between entry characteristics and outcomes are low.

Conclusion

This chapter has completed the review process of Part A. It has concluded that there has been no existing model of drop-out in distance education which has received sufficient empirical testing. The most suitable starting point towards such a model would appear to be Tinto's model for on-campus study. This model seems to be the most widely accepted of those available and has already been quite extensively cited in the distance education literature.

The chapter has begun the process of adapting Tinto's model for adult students in open learning courses. The important initial step has been the re-definition of academic and social integration to suit the nature of distance education.

The main elements of the model of student progress now appear as in Figure 4-1.

Figure 4-1: Main Elements of the Model of Student Progress

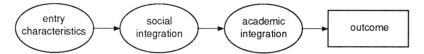

In the next part of this book each of these core elements will be elaborated upon. Sub-components of each will be introduced and explained. The model will develop from being an outline of core elements to a fuller version capable of explaining the complexity of part-time study in open learning courses.

Part B

Illustration and Explanation
of the Model

Chapter 5

Development of a Model

Synopsis

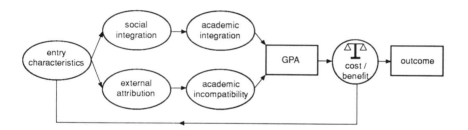

To proceed from this theoretical framework towards a tested model was an iterative process drawing upon existing qualitative research, mainly from Australia, Papua New Guinea and the United Kingdom and involving major new projects in Hong Kong and Australia utilizing both quantitative and qualitative data. The Hong Kong study developed a Distance Education Student Progress (DESP) inventory to further develop and test the model. Given the diversity of sources of input data the model can reasonably be assumed to be generic.

To accommodate initial quantitative data the framework derived in Chapter 4 was developed towards a two-track model. The positive track contains factors which lead to high levels of both social and academic integration. The negative track indicates lower levels of integration. The model contains a cost/benefit analysis step in which the student periodically weighs the benefits and costs of continuing to study. At this stage a decision can result in either dropping-out or continuing study. If the latter, a recycling loop leads to another passage through the cycle, usually with the characteristics and variables somewhat changed. If the results of the cost/benefit analyses continue to show positive benefits a student will eventually complete the course.

Preview

Proceeding from the idea of adapting Tinto's model along the lines suggested in the previous chapter to the fully developed model discussed in the remainder of this book took a few research projects spread over several years. During this time tentative models were transformed several times to accommodate research findings and developing ideas.

In Chapters 6 to 10, I make use of data gathered from these projects to illustrate and substantiate each facet of the final model. In order to make the book more logical, consistent and hopefully easier to read, I have re-interpreted all data from past projects so as to fit with the final version of the model presented in this book. References are given to papers where the data was first published, but readers examining those papers will find they refer to earlier less developed versions of the model. The data for one of the sources was actually used to interpret a quite different model.

Chapters 6 to 10 make use of qualitative data to explain each facet of the model. Direct quotations from interviews with students are used to illuminate each element of the model. Chapters 11 and 12 give the results of two separate quantitative tests of the full model. In practice the qualitative and quantitative research was inter-mingled and inter-related—each drawing inspiration and direction from the other. Hopefully, separating the presentation in this way should again make the explanation easier to follow.

Methodology

As the processes of collecting and analyzing the data and theory building took place over an extended period of time, the research approach has both inductive and deductive elements. I had been involved in research into drop-out from distance education courses for a number of years and had read the work of others in the same and related fields. This culminated in an earlier model derived from theory (Kember, 1989a). This initial theory base guided the design of the study described in this book. The open-ended questions in the interview schedule targeted topics which the theory predicted would be important.

Interview quotations have been drawn from five studies which examined a wide range of courses from more than ten institutions. The data were first examined in the context of each course. For the Hong Kong study, whole transcripts were available of 60 responses to the interview schedule given in Appendix A. These were sorted so that responses to similar questions were grouped, but with the respondents still identified. The process is akin to forming a variable-by-respondent matrix, though in this case the volume of data was far to large to portray on a two dimensional sheet. Data from the other studies were then combined at positions corresponding to appropriate questions or variables.

Having performed this initial ordering of the data, it was then possible to compare responses from all interviewees to similar questions. As the interviewees were grouped by the course or program for which they enrolled, it was also possible to perform a cross-course analysis. The technique is referred to by Miles and Huberman (1984) as cross-site analysis. The method used for the initial data sorting fits closest to their technique of analysis by an unordered meta-matrix (pp. 151-158).

The desirability of multiple comparison groups was argued by Glaser and Strauss (1967). The ability to perform cross-site or cross-course analysis is seen as particularly important in a distance education context. Most research in distance education has been confined to a single institution and often to an individual course. There has, therefore, been limited potential for developing generalizable theory and for building generic models.

Once the data had been ordered it was possible to search across interviewees and courses for common responses or constructs with respect to similar questions or variables. As a safeguard, this analysis process was performed independently by two researchers, with analysis of portions of the data by more. Categories and constructs which emerged from the data were discussed within the project team for conceptual verification. No attempt was made to categorize each and every statement into a limited number of categories. The process was more in line with seeking important conceptual insights which contribute to determining student progress. The quotations selected for this book are those which represented significant constructs which appeared across the range of projects and courses. Some quotations are used more than once as they illustrate related concepts.

The important constructs derived from the analysis were then built into a causal model using the process described by Miles and Huberman (1984, pp. 151-158). The process is one of seeing which variables are closely related and which seem to influence others. The eventual aim is an integrated set of relationships.

Theory was grounded in the data, to use the term made well-known by Glaser and Strauss (1967), in the sense that constructs were derived from the interview transcripts. Formation of the theory, though, was also influenced by the original theoretical model (Kember, 1989a), knowledge of other relevant theory and by complementary findings from quantitative data. Comparison of the theoretical model (Kember, 1989a) and that in this book, will show the influence of the model in the analysis of the data. However, the rearrangements, extensions and marked elaborations result from the fresh analysis of the interview data. As is becoming increasingly common, the research paradigm takes a middle ground between the extremes of deductivism and inductivism.

Analysis of the quantitative data used factor and item analysis to identify important factors or constructs. These were then formed into a conceptual model by regression and path analysis. This method of analyzing the data has a close parallel with that for the qualitative data. Findings from the qualitative data could then be triangulated against concepts which emerged from the analysis of the quantitative data. To make this book easy to follow, the analysis of the quantitative data is presented as a verification of the causal model derived from the quantitative data. In practice this neat separation was not possible. Qualitative and quantitative data were gathered and analyzed simultaneously over a period of more than three years. In practice the formation of models was a more interactive process in which the analysis of one form of data influenced that of the other.

As a result of seeking common constructs across such a diverse range of courses in markedly different environments, the resulting model has a generic nature and should be applicable, with some adaptation, to a wide range of other courses and contexts. By seeking common constructs across courses, the representative quotations which emerged have proved to be ones which might originate from adult students enrolled in any open learning or distance education course in virtually any country. The cases presented seem readily interpretable without recourse to detailed information about the context. The courses examined are, therefore, described to give the reader an idea of the context, but these descriptions have been kept quite brief.

Qualitative Data

To make the chapters in Part B understandable, it is necessary to give a brief outline of where the data presented in these chapters were collected. The interview quotations and case studies which underpin the presentation and explanation of the model in Chapters 6 to 10 are taken from five sources. Kennedy and Powell (1976) present cases taken from case notes by student counselors from the Open University in the United Kingdom. The students were all enrolled in degree courses offered by the Open University. Kennedy and Powell used the case notes as evidence for their own model, which was quite different from the one in this book. Cases from this source are referenced to the original paper.

The second source was from interviews of students undertaking a Matriculation Studies course at the University of Papua New Guinea. Entry to the course was restricted to those aged twenty one or more, and who had worked for at least two years. The course was designed for adults who did not have the normal level of qualifications for university entry. The course operated by a combination of distance education and intensive summer school courses.

The research project in which they were gathered has been previously described (Kember, 1981). Students were interviewed, mostly face-to-face, but a few by telephone. The interviews started with broad questions associated with the way in which students coped with part-time study at a distance and any difficulties encountered. Issues raised by the students were explored by more specific questions. The interviews were therefore not tightly structured so as to allow the students to raise the concerns which were important to them. Extracts from these case studies are cited in the following chapters as "(PNG student)".

The third source of case studies was a project at the University of Tasmania, Launceston in Australia which examined the reasons cited by students for their withdrawal from distance education courses. The project has been reported by Osborne, Kilpatrick and

Kember (1987). The courses used multi-media study packages, and most also had tutorials and/or weekend schools.

For four semesters, during the period 1983 to 1985, students who withdrew from a distance education course were sent a questionnaire. The questionnaire included a number of Likert scale responses related to potential reasons for withdrawal. Two open-ended questions inquired about reasons for withdrawal and about potential improvements to courses or services. Quotations are taken from responses to these open ended questions. Quotations taken from this project are cited as "(University of Tasmania). "

Another study conducted in Australia was by Roberts, Boyton, Buete and Dawson (1991). They interviewed distance education students at Charles Sturt University, Riverina during a residential school session. An earlier theoretical version of the model (Kember, 1989a) was used to underpin their study and the interview schedule was similar to that used in the Hong Kong study and given in Appendix A. Again, cases from this source are referenced to the original paper.

The largest source of case studies and interview quotations was a project which investigated seven open learning programs in Hong Kong. All programs were available only to adult students with three having open entry qualifications. The programs all used a media package for the delivery of instruction. Print was the predominant medium, but a variety of other media including audio and video cassettes and direct broadcast television were utilized. Each program was supported by face-to-face tutorials for groups of students. In addition, four of the programs offered telephone counseling services to answer individual student queries. One program offered a similar service by fax. A summary of the programs is given in Table 5-1. The offerings of the Open Learning Institute of Hong Kong (OLIHK) were treated as one program, despite the fact that data was gathered on courses in the arts, business and science, because the institution offers all courses to a similar academic format.

Each program was examined by a combination of qualitative and quantitative methods. Qualitative data was gathered by semi-structured interviews with 60 students randomly selected from the entire population of the seven programs. Nearly all the interviews were conducted in Cantonese by the project's research assistant. Tape recordings of the interviews were translated into

English and analyzed independently by two members of the research team. Interview responses to each question were sorted into categories. As the number of interviews was quite high, it was possible to count the number of responses in each category for some of the questions and so provide a semi-quantitative measure. Where possible categories in the interview transcript were triangulated against data from the questionnaire. Quotations used in subsequent chapters are cited as "(Hong Kong–)" and show the course in which the student was enrolled. Further details of the interviewing and analysis of the transcripts are given in Kember, Lai, Murphy, Siaw, Wong and Yuen (1990).

Quantitative Data

The Distance Education Student Progress (DESP) questionnaire was used for the quantitative analysis. A copy of the questionnaire is given in Appendix B. Chapters 11 and 12 deal with the analysis of the quantitative data. Further details of the development of the questionnaire, its interpretation and data analysis are given in Kember, Murphy, Siaw and Yuen (1991) and in Kember, Lai, Murphy, Siaw and Yuen (1992a).

The DESP inventory starts by soliciting information on 18 demographic variables. Remaining items ask students to respond on a five-point Likert scale, from definitely agree to definitely disagree. The items in the questionnaire contain statements relating to each of the components and sub-components of the model. Because English is a second language for the students in the Hong Kong study, the questionnaire was translated into Chinese, with independent back translation to check the accuracy of the translation.

The samples for the two quantitative studies were from the Hong Kong courses described in Table 5-1. The population for the original study was students from the textiles, management and taxation courses. The replication study sampled students in the student guidance and education courses, and students enrolled for Open Learning Institute courses in business, science and the arts.

Table 5-1: Programs Examined in the Hong Kong Study

Subject	Institutions	Level	Entry Qualification
Textiles	Hong Kong Polytechnic	Certificate	HKCEE or above 25 years of age
Management	Warwick University / HK Management Association / HK Polytechnic	Master's degree	First degree or 4 years management experience
Taxation	Hong Kong Polytechnic / Taxation Institute of Hong Kong	Certificate	Open
Student Guidance	Hong Kong Polytechnic	Postgraduate Diploma	Bachelor's degree, must be practicing student counselor
Business/ Science/Arts	Open Learning Institute of HK	Bachelor's Degree	Open
Law	ACCA / Hong Kong Polytechnic	ACCA Qualifying	Open
Education	Deakin University/ Chinese University/ Commercial Radio	Bachelor's degree	Teaching qualification

Table 5-1 Continued

Normal Duration	Media Package	Tutorial Support	Other Support
3 years	Print, video cassettes, practical kits	Tutorial every 4 weeks	Telephone counseling
4 years	Print	A 4.5 hour session for each subject	Telephone counseling
4 months	Print	4 times for 2 hours each	Telephone counseling
1.5 years	Print	Colloquia, workshops & tutorials about every 2 weeks	Informal contact
6 years	Print, direct Broadcast TV, plus other media	Tutorial every 2 weeks	Telephone counseling
.4 months	Print	Tutorial every 3 weeks	Fax service for queries–response by phone
2.5 years	Print, audio tapes, videotapes	Tutorial every 4 weeks	"Group of 5" study group

A Two-track Model

Factor analysis of the data collected with the DESP inventory produced factors which split both social and academic integration variables into positive and negative factors. Path analysis was consistent with the positive and negative factors appearing in discrete paths.

These results are best interpreted in terms of the two-track model which appears as Figure 5-1. This model suggests that students' entry characteristics direct them towards one of two tracks. Those with favorable situations tend to proceed on the positive track and are able to integrate socially and academically. Others take the lower, negative track where they have greater difficulties achieving social and academic integration.

The model now also includes a cost/benefit decision, during which students consider the costs and benefits of continuing academic study. Those who decide to continue will then enter the recycling loop for another passage through the model. In subsequent passages through the model initial characteristics will have altered, partly as a result of developmental charges the student experienced during the course. It is, therefore, possible to switch tracks during the recycling process.

Figure 5-1: Two-track Version of the Student Progress Model

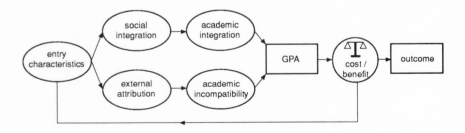

Preview

Chapters 6 to 10 explain and illustrate the various facets of the two-track model by drawing upon qualitative research. Some reference is also made to the quantitative data and in particular to scales and sub-scales which emerged from factor analysis of the questionnaire data, and to the way these inter-related in the model building process.

Chapter 6

Entry Characteristics

Synopsis

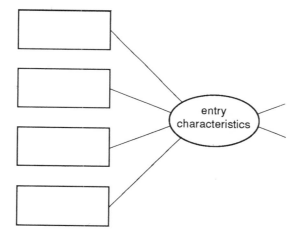

Entry characteristics were included in the model as influences upon the integration variables. There is a substantial literature, from different educational modes, on the relationship between entry characteristics and attrition. For open learning courses these studies usually have little policy relevance and do not reveal correlations of sufficient magnitude to have any value as predictors of course outcomes. However, the studies do show that student behavior in open learning courses is influenced by entry characteristics and, as such, the literature does have relevance to the model. This chapter, therefore, contains a brief review of the studies relating individual variables to persistence and discusses those most likely to influence social and academic integration.

Entry Characteristics and Persistence

In Chapter 3, I suggested that mainstream research has largely abandoned the attempt to predict college persistence from student entry characteristics or demographic data. Where significant relationships were found, they were almost invariably too small to explain much of the variance. The relationships which existed were not strong enough to predict with certainty how successful a given student would be, purely by examining enrollment data.

The relationship between entry characteristics and persistence can yield useful information even if it does not directly predict outcomes. It can be useful to know which types of students normally do better so that at-risk students can be identified and appropriate counseling adopted. There are normally some small but significant correlations between categories recorded on application forms and student progress. For example, Woodley and Parlett (1983) found that sex, age, previous educational qualifications, occupation and region of residence were all related to persistence for students enrolled with the Open University of the United Kingdom. Rekkedal (1972) related age, previous education, years of school experience and even month of enrollment with persistence. Kember (1981) found significant relationships between persistence and age, number of children, housing conditions, sex, sponsorship and region of residence.

These studies relating persistence data to individual variables can give useful information for pointing out at-risk students and for institutional evaluation and planning. However, the information normally given needs to be treated with considerable caution. Those with little understanding of statistics can easily fall into a number of common traps.

To illustrate the potential pit-falls, I will use some typical data given by Woodley, Thompson and Cowan (1992) on persistence in Scottish universities. I would hasten to add that the authors themselves did not fall into any of the traps, but in fact treated the data very intelligently.

- In five of the eight Scottish universities the leaving pattern was similar to that found elsewhere, with most non-completers leaving in the first year. In the other three, students tended to leave in the second year or later.

- Non-completion rates in Scottish universities were highest in Engineering subjects, with one in five of all entrants failing to graduate. The rates for Science were lower and for social Science and Arts lower still. The non-completion rates were lowest for Medicine and related subjects.

- Women were more likely than men to graduate.

- Students living in halls of residence in their first year were slightly more successful than those living at home but those in flats and 'digs' fared worst.

- The children of professional parents were slightly more successful than those of non-professional parents.

- Students from state and private schools were equally successful; those entering from further education were the least successful.

- There was no clear relationship with age on entry. (pp. 2-3)

Firstly, it is important to be aware that statistically significant differences result from very small discrepancies in persistence rates between categories when samples are large. For example the item showing that women are more likely to graduate than men is no doubt statistically significant but in practice the difference might be very small.

For a small course with 300 students a correlation coefficient as low as 0.148 is sufficient for significance at the 1% level and 0.113 is adequate at the 5% level accepted in most educational research (Snedecor & Cochran, 1967, p. 557). The latter level of correlation means that only 0.013% of the variance has been explained, but the correlation coefficient is quite sufficient to make the type of statements quoted above.

Even if the differences are substantial it is usually impossible or undesirable to do anything about them. Selecting female students rather than male, or vice versa, would be illegal in most countries. Giving preference to the children of professional parents would be socially unacceptable. In general, therefore, any relationships between background variables and progress are unlikely to be policy relevant, particularly for open learning and adult education courses.

The final caution is that statistical relationships do not imply causation. It may be true that drop-out is highest in the first year of a course but it is clearly ludicrous to suppose that admitting students directly to the second year is going to reduce drop-out. Similarly it may be true that engineering courses have higher drop-out rates than arts ones, but forcing students into arts courses may actually increase attrition as most students would end up in courses in which they had no interest. However, it is possible that engineering courses have high drop-out rates because they are heavily overloaded, in which case some remedial action is possible.

Including Entry Characteristics in Models

Models such as those by Spady (1971) and Tinto (1975) focused researchers' attention more towards what happens after enrollment than upon predicting success at entry. Enrollment characteristics are included in these models, but as influences upon later events rather than as direct predictors of outcomes. Similarly the model proposed in this book includes entry characteristics as its starting point. These characteristics encompass the demographic variables known on the entry of a student into a course. These variables are easily determined from application or registration forms or supplementary questionnaires. Some of the variables have been shown to have weak correlations with dropout. Their inclusion in the model is because of their influence on other components of the model rather than for these weak direct correlations.

The quotation below is used to show how individual characteristics can influence later components. The quotation is derived from a counselor's report on a student from a working class background, with limited schooling.

> A friendly but distant relationship has been built up with the counselor: the reason for the distance is undoubtedly an exaggerated mixture of respect and cautiousness which this student feels when he encounters white collar workers. He could in some circumstances, no doubt, be extremely antagonistic towards those whom he feels have a down on the working class and he is of the opinion that the Open University does not really try to enroll working class students. On the other hand, he sees the workers

cannot be readily interested in the Open University as his own
attempts to influence workmates have shown him.

In general, then, he is not easy to get through to because he feels
somewhat uncertain of his own position (jobwise) and somewhat
unsure of the position of academics who are neither bosses nor
white collar workers.

His motivation is extremely complex. No doubt it is partly intrinsic
(self-fulfillment through study), yet while it is by no means overtly
extrinsic (degree collecting), there is an element of the desire to
obtain a degree (or qualification in Music) to show that he is 'as
good as them.' (Kennedy & Powell, 1976, p. 69)

The quotation discusses the influence on goal commitment of the
student's attitudes and working class background. The
relationship with the tutor will affect the degree of academic
integration. The student will clearly find it difficult to integrate
with the academic norms of a university because of his attitude
and background. Integration of study with work life will also be
influenced by his attitudes and those of his workmates.

Educational Qualifications

The variable which is most widely used as a predictor of success
in educational courses is past educational attainments. The
variable is not only used as a predictor but also as a qualification
required for entry and as a selection tool for choosing between
competing entrants. Traditionally students are denied entry to a
program until they have graduated from the preceding level of
education. Where places are restricted they are normally awarded
to those with the best examination results from the preceding
level.

The relationship between educational background and
persistence and performance has been widely researched. Grade
performance in high school has been shown to be related to
college performance by studies such as those by Blanchfield
(1971), Chase (1970), Jaffe and Adams (1970), Lavin (1965), Panos
and Astin (1968), and Taylor and Hanson (1970). However, the
correlations between final high-school grades and degree class
are usually in the region of 0.20, (Entwistle & Ramsden, 1983, p.
33) statistically significant but explaining only a very small
proportion of the variance.

When mature students are involved, the link between school results and college or university performance is even more tenuous. Students rarely enroll in open learning courses straight from high school. They are more normally mature students with several, or sometimes many, intervening years between leaving school and commencing their open learning course. In that time a rich variety of experience may have contributed to their ability to tackle a college course. On the other hand, some mature entrants leave school early and their subsequent experiences provide little additional preparation for academic study. The quotations below show that some students take advantage of open entry policies to enroll in open learning courses, having been unable to gain entry to other courses with formal entry requirements.

> The minimum requirement to enroll into this distance learning course is unrestricted, unlike other clothing and textiles diploma courses which usually require the minimum requirement of form 5 standard plus 3 passes in Physics, Chemistry and Biology. With my limited qualifications I am only eligible to do this distance learning course. Moreover I don't intend to give up my full-time job, therefore, I think this distance learning course is suitable for me. (Hong Kong–Textiles)

> I enrolled in this distance learning course because I was rejected by the Technical Institute for the third time. I felt like giving up applying to Technical Institutes anymore. Since the courses offered by Technical Institute are more or less equivalent to those offered in the Polytechnic and I think the chance of acceptance should be higher, therefore, I tried to apply here. (Hong Kong–Textiles)

> Because I was rejected by any other tertiary institutions except OLI. Also I wish to obtain a degree. (Hong Kong–OLIHK)

The widespread existence of mature entry programs indicates that mature students, without the formal qualifications required of high school graduates, can and do succeed in higher education. Not many distance education institutions have published data comparing the performance of "unqualified" mature entrants with students who possess the normal formal entry qualifications. Where studies have been completed, the findings usually show that the mature entrants do not perform quite as well as traditionally qualified entrants, but the mature entrants do perform well enough to justify the existence and continuance of the special conditions associated with the mature entry program (Kember, 1982).

By no means all of the students in open learning courses, though, are traditionally unqualified. In fact there is a growing trend for graduates to enroll in open learning courses because of continuing education needs. As the pace of technological change quickens, this trend is likely to grow. Such students clearly choose open learning because it offers them freedom as to where and when they study. They can be part-time students so are able to maintain employment.

> I would still prefer distance learning because I don't have to give up my full-time job. Full-time education is obviously not possible for me since there is no income for me. (Hong Kong–Textiles)

The relationship between educational background and persistence is unlikely to have a strong direct causal link to student progress. Educational background is, however, included in the initial stage of the model. It is present because educational background can influence other components of the linear model, rather than for any direct relationship with drop-out. The quotation given in the previous section is a prime example of how difficult academic integration can become when students have limited previous education.

The educational facet of the characteristics component needs some care in interpretation. The information, which is readily available and most normally used, is the results in formal (normally school-level) examinations undertaken by students. Such data may not be highly relevant for mature students who left high school some years previously. More recent data on educational aptitude, common to all entrants, can only be included if applicants are subjected to some form of testing by the institution. Few institutions currently perform such tests presumably because of questions over difficulties of administration, validity of testing, and negation of social and political open access goals. It is therefore likely that the only available data, relating to educational background, will be the formal school qualifications or examination results.

It seems worthwhile using such data in the model but viewing the information as an influence on later components of the model rather than predictors of success or barriers for entry to the course. Students with less formal schooling and little history of study since leaving school are likely to face more problems with academic integration than those who have had a thorough exposure to the processes of study either at or since leaving school. Students with a limited history of schooling are less likely to have developed a study approach which is compatible with the demands of tertiary education. They are unlikely to be conversant with the conventions and norms of academic life. Success is unlikely unless the students' work is congruent with these academic norms.

Family Status

I feel sure that those with children firmly believe that study in the home, and many more tasks beside, would be easier without them. It is not difficult to accept that the following students will find greater difficulties with an open learning course:

> I have a husband and three children, 7, 5 and 3. They are very demanding and reliant. (Roberts, Boyton, Buete & Dawson, 1991, p. 78)

> I have my wife, my mother, my son and 3 younger sisters staying with me. (Hong Kong–Taxation)

than students like this one:

> I live with my husband. (Hong Kong–Student Guidance)

There are normally slightly better completion rates for those without children, but as for other demographic variables the differences are very small. Students with several young children, living in small houses, can and do complete open learning courses, while being without family obligations is certainly no guarantee of success.

The influence of family status may not be as clear-cut as might be expected as it can interact with the age of the students. More mature students can perform slightly better than their younger counterparts for several reasons. Older students, though, are more likely to have children so the two effects can cancel each other out to some extent.

Family status variables are, therefore, not included in the model as direct predictors of student progress, but as indicators of the degree of social integration which will be necessary. Those with young children will have to find a place and a time to study free from the potential distractions of the children. The family unit will have to determine a balance between time spent on study, with children and on other tasks and pleasures. Those without children need to determine how to cope with the additional demands of part-time study while still maintaining relationships with partners and colleagues.

Chapter 7 shows how students can adapt to apparently adverse family situations. Chapter 8, though, suggests that failure to integrate family obligations with study requirements is likely to place students at-risk.

Employment

Many students enroll in courses largely because they wish to further their careers. The employment situation can, therefore, provide motivation and stimulation to progress in a course. On the other hand, the working week devours much of an employee's available time. Time at work is in direct competition with time to study. Work obligations are frequently cited by those who have been unable to spend sufficient time studying.

> I am a manager in a garment company. My job nature is mainly dealing with office management and making business contacts with prospective buyers. My normal working hours are from 9 to 5 but there is usually overtime. For the sake of business, I frequently have to travel to China, South-East Asia, Macau, etc. (Hong Kong–Textiles)

Unlike some other variables, it is not easy to find a simple measure which directly compares work demands. Two people in apparently similar positions can face quite different situations.

> I am working as a Sales Executive but mostly I am dealing with the job of coordination. Our regular working hours are from 8:30 am to 5:15 pm. Our company tries not to have overtime work for the employees. If there is excess work, the company will recruit new employees. So far I don't have to go for business trips. (Hong Kong–Textiles)

These contrasting situations could only have been fully exposed by qualitative approaches. To provide a convenient usable variable for the quantitative test of the model, salary was used. Those with higher salaries tend to have greater responsibilities and obligations.

Salary can also be an indicator of a student's ability to pay course fees. Open learning courses often require students to pay substantial course fees and these do affect students motivation. Tinto (1987) claims that few full-time college students drop-out purely because they are unable to afford course fees. The same may be true of students in open learning courses. Course fees do, though, have a profound effect on the motivation of some students as will become apparent over the next few chapters.

> My study does affect my family in that the school fees are expensive. (Hong Kong–Textiles)

Other Variables

The DESP inventory, used for the quantitative tests of the model described in Chapters 11 and 12, sought a range of demographic information from students. This information proved valuable in building a picture of the type of students enrolling in the open learning courses concerned (Kember, Lai, Murphy, Siaw & Yuen, 1992b).

Demographic information can be helpful to administrators for planning student support services and when seeking to recruit students. It can be useful to faculty when courses are designed to have information about the nature of students who will take their courses. Tutors find it helpful to know something about the students with whom they will have to interact.

For reasons such as these, gathering demographic or enrollment data is a useful exercise. It does not imply, though, that this information will have a marked bearing on student progress. The majority of the demographic information from the DESP inventory was not included in the eventual model of student progress. The variables which were included had statistical links to the integration variables described in the next three chapters, but statistically significant links to outcome measures were few and far between.

Conclusion

Background information on students is important as a starting point. The characteristics, demographic status, educational background and experience of students will play a major part in determining how well the students are able to achieve academic and social integration. Knowledge of students' entry characteristics should help tutors and counselors acclimatize to academic study.

It should be stressed, though, that entry characteristics are just a starting point in determining how much difficulty a student is likely to face in coping with a course. Many students with apparently adverse circumstances do succeed. Entry characteristics are not good predictors of final outcomes.

Chapter 7

Social Integration

Synopsis

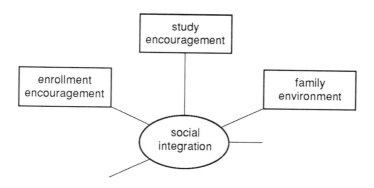

Adult part-time students cannot eschew existing work, family and social obligations by completing a rite of passage and become a full-time student. The new, and often taxing, demands of academic study must be accommodated alongside these on-going commitments. The social integration construct examines the degree to which students are able to integrate their academic study with the often conflicting employment, family and social requirements.

Integration

Students enrolled in open learning courses are normally part-time students. They could well be in full-time employment. They may have a family to support and look after. They will be meshed in an existing social network. On becoming students they will not be able to undergo a rite of passage and leave behind all these

79

existing commitments and obligations. The home, social and work environment remains important in distance education as study normally takes place in the home and most students have a full-time job to complement or conflict with their study.

They will have to mesh the role of a part-time student into their lives, which normally means some degree of adaptation to their existing lifestyle. The social integration component of the model deals with the degree to which a student is able to integrate the study process with work, family and social life.

The social integration component in the model is influenced by the entry characteristics relating to work, the home and the social environment. Students with any adverse characteristics, in this domain, will have greater difficulties in integrating the demands of study into the home environment. The attitudes of family, employers, workmates and social colleagues are important in determining the success of integrating study into their daily lives. If these attitudes are sufficiently supportive, apparently adverse circumstances can be overcome.

This chapter looks at the difficulties students have in achieving social integration and the ways in which more successful students are able to overcome an apparently adverse environment. The chapter is divided into sections corresponding to the three sub-components of the social integration component of the model. Each sub-component is illustrated by interview quotations from the various qualitative studies. Each of the sub-components has a quantitative counterpart consisting of a sub-scale in the DESP instrument. The three sub-components are listed below.

- Enrollment encouragement examines the extent to which the employer, family and friends supported the student's decision to enroll in the course. Such initial support has an important bearing upon goal commitment.

- Study encouragement considers the degree of co-operation and moral support the student receives when actually studying.

- The family environment sub-scale determines whether a warm supporting environment exists within the family unit.

The sections are further divided into sub-sections corresponding to the work, home and social environments. These are the major spheres of influence upon the part-time students. In a few cases all three of these environments may not be relevant or important.

Enrollment Encouragement

The enrollment encouragement sub-scale indicates encouragement for the student to enroll in the course. A positive attitude from others at the enrollment stage helps a student to enter a course in a positive, confident frame of mind. If the employer and family are committed and supportive of a student enrolling in a course, it suggests that they will be facilitative in the subsequent social integration process and could be supportive when difficulties are encountered.

Work

The quotations below are typical of employer encouragement. These students will enter their courses knowing that they have strong support from an important source. There is something of an obligation to do well. As the course progresses, there could be further support from the employer.

> Actually I was not the one to take the initiative. My principal encouraged me to apply as I am involved in counseling this year. When I think about my present work role, I think it will be useful to know more about counseling. (Hong Kong–Student Guidance)

> I enrolled in this course because my company encouraged me to apply. (Hong Kong–Taxation)

The next quotation shows the influence of a negative attitude from an employer.

> I now work for P.... They will not sponsor me. They sponsor sporting events but not education for their staff. I now work seven days a week which does not leave much time for study. (PNG student)

The student knew that it was quite common for other employers to sponsor their students on the course in question. The attitude of this employer in rating sporting events as a higher priority than the education of employees is obviously a sore point. It means that there was a negative element in the mind of the student even as the course started. Incidentally, the employer's attitude seems unlikely do much for employee productivity either.

Family

It is important that a family encourages a student to enroll in a course. The student will then see that they perceive benefits from the course and the eventual qualification it will bring. Once the course starts, the student should be able to envisage that study will be treated as a priority. If family members are ambivalent or even hostile towards the student enrolling in a course, they will eventually see time spent studying as a competing event to activities they currently enjoy with the student.

> They encouraged me to enroll and part of the financial support was from them. (Hong Kong–OLIHK)

The student who made the above comment can clearly see that the family (they) are committed to the course in question. Such initial encouragement and involvement could do much to spur the student towards successful outcomes.

Study Encouragement

The study encouragement sub-scale corresponds to support from the same sources, of workplace, family and social circle, once the course is in operation. When study commences the student realizes just what the demands of part-time study are like. It is the time when existing patterns of life need to be modified to allow time to be committed to study. Fellow workers, family and friends can either support the adjustment process or can be a major impediment to integration. For part-time study to be successfully assimilated, it is likely that those in the student's immediate environment will have to make some adaptation too.

Work

Integration with employment will depend on the attitude of employer and workmates. Some employers are highly supportive of study and allow time from work for study or activities such as residential schools. Others appear indifferent, and some are even hostile, presumably seeing study as a drain of potential energies which might be devoted to work. The attitude of the employer is important in reinforcing the student's goal commitment. A strengthening of extrinsic motivation will occur if the employer makes it clear that successful completion of the course will lead to rewards, such as promotion. The following quotation shows how a supportive employer assisted a student, who was a laboratory technician, to integrate study demands with work requirements.

> We usually get all the analyses completed in the morning. If there are problems with the plant we work on those in the afternoon. But if the plant is running smoothly there is often little work in the afternoon. The boss directs the other technicians to do the jobs which need doing, leaving the students free to work on their studies.

> I also go into work on Saturdays to study. If I stay at home someone always comes round to invite me out for a beer or to play snooker. I also have two children at home who interfere with work. (PNG student)

The supportive attitude of the employer must not only have aided the integration process but would surely increase goal commitment too. The employer's actions would leave little doubt that the course of study was considered valuable. By contrast the next group of quotations from the study in Australia of Roberts, Boyton, Buete and Dawson (1991) shows that many students face indifferent or hostile employers.

> Most senior staff are supportive but Board members are antagonistic.

> Matron is not impressed.

> The boss wouldn't even know I'm studying—I use my sick leave to come to residential schools.

> I had to resign from my hospital in ... because they refused to grant me leave to come to residential schools. (Roberts, Boyton, Buete & Dawson, 1991, p. 77)

The latter two comments above refer to residential schools. These were compulsory sessions lasting for a few days when students attend the main campus for classes. Students can obviously find the attendance requirement a problem if their employer is uncooperative. Indifferent or hostile employers provide no help with providing study time or assistance, but go further than this in de-motivating the student.

> I didn't get much help from my employer. The work involves traveling round to repair equipment and it's difficult to study when traveling, especially if you have to go into the bush. (PNG student)

The attitudes of workmates can also influence integration of the student into the study habit. Supportive fellow workers will encourage the student, but if co-workers pour scorn on the idea of spending time on study then the student will clearly be discouraged.

> Luckily my course is related to my job. My senior colleague always distributes useful counseling handouts to me and keeps me informed of certain useful workshops to attend. I also have my spare time to go over the course materials. (Hong Kong–Student Guidance)

Sometimes workmates can sympathize with the student but find it difficult to provide any concrete assistance.

> Most of the time I put the school work in the first priority. Looking at the view point of our school administration, I realize that it is difficult to release me from the heavy workload because it won't be fair to other teachers who have to take over part of my workload. (Hong Kong–Student Guidance)

The school administration may not be able to release the student, but at least the student does not face a negative attitude. Colleagues can, at least, offer moral encouragement and show interest. The student making the comment below clearly faces a far more discouraging situation.

> My colleagues think I'm eccentric! (Roberts, Boyton, Buete & Dawson, 1991, p. 77)

Family

The immediate family is another major factor in the degree of congruence of the study process with the student's life style. If family members see the eventual qualification and the need for study as an important aspect of their interests then they are likely to support the student in spending time on study activities. If, however, the family perceives family duties as having priority over study time, then it will be difficult to smoothly integrate periods of study with the family lifestyle.

A supportive family will be willing to make changes to their lifestyle to facilitate the study process. These changes can range from quite minor ones to learning to sleep with the light on.

> When I am studying at home, my husband has to put on the headphones when watching TV. (Hong Kong–Law)

> I affect them if I want to study at midnight with the light on when everyone is sleeping. However, this effect is only a minor one as they get used to it. (Hong Kong–Textiles)

Children are usually seen as an impediment to study. Child care is one activity which often has to take priority over study, particularly when children are young. It can then be particularly helpful if a spouse or other members of a family are willing to take over child care duties to allow time for study or attending classes.

> My study doesn't affect them much except when I have to attend tutorials, the other family members will have to take care of my child. Distance learning is better than part-time study for which I would have to ask other family members to take care of the child regularly as the part-time classes used to be held at least one to two times a week. (Hong Kong–Taxation)

Friends and Fellow Students

In this component of the model, congruence of the study process with the student's social life has to be taken into account. A hectic social life or social contacts who deride time spent studying would hinder integration of the study process into the student's life. Friends, though, can be an important source of help with a course. The provision of help can do much for motivation as well as assisting understanding.

> My friends do affect my study in the sense that we can interchange new ideas in the garment field. Therefore, with wider knowledge, we definitely improve our point of view. (Hong Kong–Textiles)

> So far, I feel lucky because I have many friends who are working in the same field as mine. Whenever I encounter any difficulty dealing

with taxation, I can always get it solved easily through discussion with my friends. (Hong Kong–Taxation)

Help and motivation can come from fellow students as well as from workmates. The quotation below is from a student enrolled in a course which made a point of trying to get students to meet together in small groups of about five students, independently of a tutor. The quotation suggests that the strategy can be very effective.

Yes, I felt discouraged and frustrated and often came close to giving it up when I worked on my first assignment. Luckily the support from my group kept me to stay in the course. I knew that I wasn't the only person to have problems in the first assignment, there were the same problems faced by my group mates as well. Now, I do not have the feeling of giving it up since I understand its learning approach—free thinking. (Hong Kong–Education)

Family Support

The family support sub-scale is indicative of a warm supportive environment within the family. It indicates a family which has sufficient cohesiveness to accept the inevitable perturbations which arise when a member of the family becomes a part-time student. These changes to the family members will inevitably act against the individual interests of some members of the family so the difficulty and degree of sacrifice and adaptation should not be underestimated. The quotation below is typical of many families, yet it is also indicative of a family which will need to adapt in a supporting manner if the student is to be successful.

I have a husband and three children, 7, 5 and 3. They are very demanding and reliant. (Roberts, Boyton, Buete & Dawson, 1991, p. 78)

It is inevitable that difficulties will emerge between family members at times during a course. The majority of these tensions will be manifest in a degree of conflict or tension between family members.

I find I get crotchety with the kids. (Roberts, Boyton, Buete & Dawson, 1991, p. 78)

> The kids and I get stressed before exams—I'm separated. (Roberts, Boyton, Buete & Dawson, 1991, p. 78)

More concrete strains such as depleted finances can also occur.

> Study has priority over my landscaping business, hence income has dropped, which in turn affects my family. (Roberts, Boyton, Buete & Dawson, 1991, p. 78)

The supportive family is the one which copes with these strains by adapting its routines so that there is a time and a place for study. Family members take on additional responsibilities to give the student free time to study.

> Oh yes, my husband has to do extra housework for me. (Hong Kong–Student Guidance)

They need to negotiate sanctuaries or periods of time when the student is not to be disturbed.

> School or home. They are good places to study but it is a bit harsh to my children because I won't allow them to come in my room while I am studying. (Hong Kong–Student Guidance)

The quote above suggests that a balance has to be maintained between the need for study time and the desire to maintain family relationships. An equilibrium position must be sought which allows study to progress but which also allows for the maintenance of family relationships. Almost inevitably there will have to be sacrifices from the ideal position on both sides, and it is indicative of a supporting family environment that such sacrifices are made.

> Study plays hell with my sex life! (Roberts, Boyton, Buete & Dawson, 1991, p. 78)

> Yes, I have a husband only. He tolerates my study—often he says I'm spending more times with my books than him. (Roberts, Boyton, Buete & Dawson, 1991, p. 78)

In addition to negotiating a sanctuary and a designated time for study, the accommodating family is also likely to negotiate an inviolate time for preserving family time and relationships.

> I study during weekdays so we still can have family days during weekends. (Hong Kong–OLIHK)

Conclusion

Many students face quite a difficult time in trying to integrate study requirements with what appear to be conflicting demands from work, home and friends. The environment can seem most unfavorable as the students have to fit in a niche for studying on top of what may have been an already full life.

Support from employers, work colleagues, family and friends definitely makes a difference to the success or otherwise of the integration process. The instances of successful integration given in this chapter have usually resulted from a re-negotiation of previously accepted social positions and status. In most instances the newly negotiated position results in sacrifices by the student, and often too by others in the student's social environment.

Social integration can be achieved, even in the face of an inhospitable social environment, if a time and space for study are negotiated. In the next chapter we see that this does not always happen. Those on the negative track can fail to achieve social integration.

Chapter 8

External Attribution

Synopsis

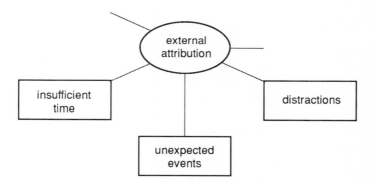

Autopsy studies of student attrition solicit direct explanations from those who dropped-out. Reasons given almost invariably cite some external cause of which "insufficient time" seems to be the most common. Such external attributions are understandable, given the framework provided by attribution theory. Those who are successful tend to accept credit by internalizing responsibility for the successful outcome. By contrast less successful ventures are easier to accept if causation is attributed to something external to the control of the individual.

Lack of social integration is frequently manifest in the student resorting to external attribution. Failure to find ways to integrate study with on-going commitments means that it is easy to blame the competing work, family and social pressures for the lack of integration.

External Attribution

It has been common to ask students withdrawing from open learning courses for the reason for their discontinued study. Sheath (1965) listed the most common reasons collected by one institution over a period of one year. The most frequent reasons given for student initiated withdrawal were as follows (p. 27):

- Insufficient time for study because of occupational or other commitments.

- Illness of student or family.

- Financial difficulties.

- Housing and accommodation difficulties.

Since this time others such as Idle (1980) and Store and Osborne (1979) have conducted similar surveys, which are often referred to as "autopsy" studies. The results of these subsequent studies invariably produce lists with great affinity to that produced by Sheath. Each of the reasons commonly given for withdrawal attributes the reason to a factor external to the control of the student. If anyone were to ask graduating students for the reason for their success, no doubt most, if not all, would give reasons corresponding to internal control, such as hard work, perseverance or cleverness.

This distinction was predicted and explained by attribution theory (Bar-Tal, 1978; Weiner, 1972; 1974). Those who do not complete a course prefer to attribute their withdrawal to factors outside their control so as to salvage some self-esteem. Those who succeed prefer to point to internal causes so as to enhance their self-esteem.

The previous chapter looked at students who succeeded at social integration: those who managed to integrate the demands of study with their private, family, social and work environment. This chapter considers students who have been less successful in the process of integrating study demands with social obligations. These students will eventually attribute their integration failure to external factors which are essentially beyond their control.

The negative social integration component is, therefore, called external attribution and is sub-divided into three sub-components, each of which has a sub-scale in the DESP inventory.

The three sub-components correspond to three of the reasons most commonly advanced by withdrawing students.

- Insufficient time is the most common reason given for drop-out in autopsy reports and indicates a failure to come to terms with competing priorities.

- Distractions attributes lack of application to study tasks to competing demands from family, employers and friends. It is indicative of a lack of social integration between academic demands and daily life.

- Events hinder study examines the way in which happenings not foreseen at the time of enrollment influence the cost-benefit analysis between continuing and ceasing study.

Insufficient Time

Of the sub-components making up the external attribution component, insufficient time is probably the most frequently cited reason for withdrawing from a course (e.g., Idle, 1980; Store & Osborne, 1979). The attribution is clearly external as it begs the question as to why other students with as many or more work and social commitments succeeded with the course.

Work

For those in full-time employment, work normally has the largest time allocation of any single activity, possibly ranking at about the same level as sleeping, about which little can be done. Work is, then, the greatest competitor for time with study. It is, therefore, inevitable that work time and pressure is among the most frequently cited reasons for discontinuing a course.

> I seldom can submit my assignment punctually. Again, every December of the year is the busiest month for the garment business and unfortunately the exam usually falls in the following month, i.e. January. For big volume business companies, we find that it is very hard to find adequate time for revision before the exam. (Hong Kong–Textiles)

The extent to which the work situation conflicts with study can be ranged on a spectrum. In the previous chapter there were some quotations from students who saw the workplace as a positive influence upon their study. Some students received help or encouragement from colleagues at work. A few students were allowed time to study during normal working hours. Others were able to use their office or workplace as a convenient place for study. Moving away from the positive end of the spectrum, the extent to which the employment situation can be justified as a negative influence depends upon the demands placed upon the employee. The longer the hours a student is expected to work, the less time available for study. The nature of the work is also important as greater stress and responsibility, or physically demanding work, leave less energy for study. Employment which requires travel, business entertaining or the like can be more disruptive than a regular routine.

Students will, therefore, experience a spectrum of demands from their workplace. Some clearly face greater time conflicts than others. What is interesting is that there is often only a limited correlation between the extent of these demands and measures of persistence. Students required to work long hours in demanding positions can and do complete open learning courses. The ones who do succeed with their courses in spite of heavy work commitments are those who take responsibility for their own scheduling and ensure that, of the time not eaten up by employment demands, sufficient is devoted to study.

Family

The other major competitor for study time is the family. Again students face a spectrum of competing demands. In general those with larger families have more foci competing for attention. Younger children can be particularly demanding, seemingly needing almost constant care.

> I have a husband and three children, 7, 5 and 3. They are very demanding and reliant. (Roberts, Boyton, Buete & Dawson, 1991, p. 78)

The previous chapter contains quotations from students whose family units coped with such situations. They were able to set aside a sanctuary for study or a time slot was negotiated for study purposes. Other family members took on extra responsibilities to give the student time and space for study. The net effects of these arrangements was usually some sacrifice of time with the family.

> I used to go out with them for morning tea on Saturday mornings. When there is any class to be held on Saturday, I then have less time to spend with them since I am busy during the weekdays. (Hong Kong–Student Guidance)

> I have less family time with them. (Hong Kong–OLIHK)

> I spend less time with my family especially when the exam is drawing near. (Hong Kong–Law)

By participating in these negotiated arrangements the family members themselves also make sacrifices in support of their student member.

> When I have to work on my assignment, I have to ask them to keep away from me. Sometimes, I feel sorry for my husband because I spend too much time on my work and study. (Hong Kong–Student Guidance)

Friends

The influence of friends is usually less marked than that of work and family as social arrangements are less binding than family ties or employment contracts. Nevertheless, some students do use social obligations as excuses for not being able to work on courses.

> Yes. I can't reject my friends' invitation to go out as it is rather difficult and childish if I give them the reason that I can't go out because I have to study at home. (Hong Kong–OLIHK)

Others recognize that sacrifices are necessary and are prepared to make them.

> I have to sacrifice my football time on Sunday mornings because that is now becoming the tutorial time. (Hong Kong–OLIHK)

> I have to disappoint a lot of my friends by not going out. (Hong Kong–Education)

> At first I thought I would be able to keep my social life unchanged, but now I know I have to sacrifice a lot in my social life. (Hong Kong–Education)

Some compensate for reductions in socializing, to some extent, by the increased social contacts with fellow students.

> In my social life, to some extent, I will increase meeting with the present classmates but decrease meeting with ordinary friends. I will try to avoid any unnecessary entertainment which is not related to my study. (Hong Kong–Textiles)

Distractions

Even when time is available, students face distractions and alternative activities competing for their attention. Lewis (1988) conducted a study of married women with children who were re-entering higher education after a break of several years. She commented upon the tensions posed by the multiple roles.

> Many returning women are pulled in several (and often conflicting) directions by a seemingly endless stream of demands from work, family, friends and community. (Lewis, 1988, p. 7)

Students enrolled in open learning courses are often at a stage in their lives when they face heavy responsibilities and commitments even before they decide to enroll in a course. Study adds another source of demands.

Work

There are some who find it difficult to constrain work requirements within what might be considered to be a normal working week. More demanding roles have a magnified effect in that they can leave students drained of energy and enthusiasm to study in the time they have left after work.

> I only have 50% confidence to succeed in this distance learning course. The frequent overseas travel, which takes up nearly two weeks of every month, and the report writing on the business trips are the main hindrance to my study. I become so tired and reluctant to study anymore after a whole day's work. (Hong Kong–Textiles)

Family and Home

The home and family circumstances influence drop-out from distance education courses because it is the home in which most study occurs. The home may not have a suitable physical environment for study.

> Yes, my family do affect my study very much. Besides taking care of my little child, I have to tolerate the television noise and the endless telephone conversation. That's why it is impossible to concentrate on my study at home. Family problems have been a hindrance to my study. (Hong Kong–Taxation)

As well as illustrating the difficulty of studying in a noisy environment, the above quotation hints at the problems which can be encountered when the home is shared with a number of other people. The problem can be particularly acute if there are young children or large or extended families sharing limited accommodation. Integration is possible, though.

> My house is like a one-room studio apartment for myself, my wife and our one child. It is not ideal for study but my wife is a teacher and she has to study too, so we study together in the evening. (PNG student)

To say that a one-room studio apartment with three occupants is not ideal for study is an understatement. However, because of the support of the wife, even these adverse circumstances can be overcome. The goal commitment must be strong. Even if the home is not particularly suitable some students find there are particular time slots when they can study at home.

> I study at home which is the only place I can use. It is difficult to concentrate at home, so I only study when my family members are all asleep. (Hong Kong–OLIHK)

Others find alternative places where study is possible. This can be in study centers provided for this specific purpose.

> I used to study in the self-study rooms which are set up by the Regional Urban Council. I do not have other choice of study place because my home is too small for study. (Hong Kong–OLIHK)

> I study in the OLI's self-study room. I do not study at home because it is noisy. Even though I have my own room at home, I still find that the TV noise disturbs me a lot. (Hong Kong–OLIHK)

I usually study in the library or in the public study center. I can't
concentrate on my study at home due to my daughter's
disturbances. As a matter of fact, I am easily influenced by the
surrounding environment. The library environment makes it easier
to concentrate. (Hong Kong–Law)

Others find the office or workplace can be used as a study venue.

I study in the office in the early morning time or after working
hours. My home is a good place for study but there are a lot of
temptations such as TV programs. (Hong Kong–OLIHK)

Still others find a variety of other venues.

Since my home is small and noisy all the time, I always study in the
fast food restaurant while having my dinner. (Hong Kong–OLIHK)

I study at the canteen in Jubilee Sports Centre. It is in fact a good
place for study because it is quiet in the afternoon. This place is
good for our group meeting as well because there are four of us
living in Shatin. (Hong Kong–Education)

There are also students who allocate both a place and a time slot
for study purposes.

I go to the library once or twice a week, usually Saturday or
Sunday. I study at home at other times. It is a good place to study at
home. (Hong Kong–OLIHK)

I am only able to spare time to study when I am taking the MTR
train in the morning and evening, or during the lunch hour break. It
is impossible to study at home because I have to take care of my
two year old little child. (Hong Kong–Taxation)

Friends

Almost all students are faced by demands and pressure from
friends which conflict with the need to spend time studying.
Those with sufficiently high levels of goal commitment seem to
find ways to overcome these pressure and integrate study time
into their lifestyle. This student clearly has a lower level of goal
commitment.

My friends do affect my study because they like to invite me to play
mahjong. (Hong Kong–Taxation)

Others cope with the conflicting social environment as was noted in the previous chapter. Better still, some build their social relationships into their lives as students.

> In fact there are some friends studying the same course with me. (Hong Kong–Education)

Unexpected Events

The two attributions dealt with so far in this chapter can occur through all or most of a course. The unexpected events sub-component deals with problems which occur for shorter durations. Students have attributed blame for drop-out or poor performance to events or circumstances which they did not anticipate when enrolling in the course. Events typically cited are illness, family or personal problems, and work demands.

Work

Taking a degree by part-time study can take six or more years. This time period is quite sufficient for substantial changes in employment conditions.

> Mr L. aged 36. A shift work maintenance engineer. He was working a three day week in January. His financial situation became serious. Since then he has worked extremely long hours to recoup his financial situation. He also works shifts. His academic work has suffered. (Case A, Kennedy & Powell, 1976, p. 71)

In the case of Mr L. the time taken up by working long hours reduced the time available for study. The combination of long hours and shift work is likely to tire him so that he studies at less than peak efficiency. The nature of the work can be important as well as the hours.

> My work affects my study when I was transferred to another department which requires a lot of outdoor work. I felt very tired after work. (Hong Kong–OLIHK)

Family

Within the family environment, health of family members seems to be the event mentioned most often. It can be the student who is ill and does not feel capable of studying.

> Before starting the course, I had 100% confidence about my ability to succeed as a distance learning student but now the confidence has dropped to 50% and this is mainly due to my bad health and family problems. (Hong Kong–Taxation)

It can also be a family member who is ill meaning that the student needs to spend time caring for the family member rather than studying. Having illness in the family can also create worry which makes it difficult to concentrate on academic study.

> The work volume for the assignment is heavy due to some recent unforeseen family circumstances such as a child's illness and house moving. (Hong Kong–Education)

> I have a husband and three kids. Sickness is my main problem–one of us always seems to be sick. Sometimes I feel I'm neglecting the kids. (Roberts, Boyton, Buete & Dawson, 1991, p. 78)

Conclusion

Chapters 7 and 8 have contrasted the social integration process along the two tracks. Along the positive track students were able to negotiate arrangements with family, friends, workmates and employers so that study could be accommodated into the pattern of their lives. Those on the negative track may have started with a less favorable situation. Those who were unable to harmonize the requirement of their course with their social setting tend to blame elements within their social environment for their resulting problems.

The degree of social integration will influence the next major component in the model, which is that for academic integration. Those who succeed with social integration will advance along the positive track in a good position to cope with the need to achieve academic integration. Those who have had difficulty with social integration are poorly positioned with respect to academic integration. They may find it hard to get off the negative track.

Chapter 9

Academic Integration or Incompatibility

Synopsis

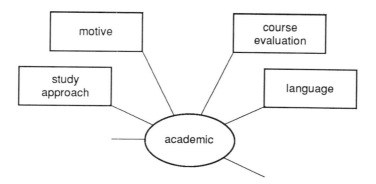

Academic integration is interpreted as encompassing all facets of a course and all elements of contact between an institution and the students whether these are of an academic, administrative or social nature. Drawing upon Durkheim's theory of suicide, integration can then take two forms. Collective affiliation can be developed in a variety of ways, such as interaction between tutors and students, or by good impressions created by efficient operations. There is also a need for moral or value integration between the academic conventions and norms of the institution and the perceptions and performance of the student.

The model splits academic integration into the positive and negative tracks. The positive variable is named academic integration while the negative variant is called academic incompatibility. Each contains four aspects or sub-scales measuring: study approach, motivation, course evaluation and language ability.

The Academic Environment

In Chapter 4 the definitions of academic and social environment were established for the model. As the teaching usually takes place at a distance, the academic setting is constructed rather differently to that for full-time students. For the open learner the predominant image of the course could well be that of a study package delivered though the mail. Contacts with faculty may not be that frequent and probably take place largely by telephone, video link, mail, or computer message. There can be as many or more interchanges with and receipts from administrators as there are with faculty.

In the model everything touching on this teaching and support environment is deemed to be part of the academic sphere. This then comprises all elements within the study package. It encompasses all contacts, face-to-face or by various media, with faculty, administrators and fellow students whether for study, administrative or social purposes.

Academic Integration or Incompatibility

The concept of integration is then introduced as the degree to which the student is able to empathize with this academic environment and to accommodate the demands of the university or college. In Durkheim's (1961) model, suicide is more likely to occur if at least one of two forms of integration is lacking, namely insufficient collective affiliation or insufficient moral or value integration; that is, low normative congruence.

To encourage persistence both sides should be seeking to develop a sense of belonging between the student and the institution. Given that most of the study normally takes place at a distance this can be a demanding task. Collective affiliation is often seen as a product of personal contact, yet a distance education student can proceed through a course without any direct contact with either faculty or fellow students.

Normative congruence can be seen as the degree of fit between the student's and the institution's expectations of each other. Universities and colleges have formal expectations posed as assignments, tests and examinations. Faculty may have expectations about these examinations and assignments which are not explicitly stated. Colleges also have less explicit expectations of students in the form of academic norms and conventions.

To determine whether a student was successfully integrated in an academic sense would require examination of each of the facets of the academic environment. Undoubtedly, some students will integrate well with one facet but not with another. In some cases the good facet will compensate for the one with poor fit, but in others a lack of integration of one facet might be a major influence towards a decision to drop out.

Academic integration and academic incompatibility are parallel scales. Each scale contains an approach to studying sub-scale, a motivation sub-scale, a sub-scale concerned with language ability or reading habits, and a sub-scale which seeks students' evaluation of the course. Each of these components or sub-scales will be considered in turn. In both cases the approach to study and motivation sub-scales of the DESP inventory were adapted from the Approaches to Studying Inventory (ASI) (Entwistle & Ramsden, 1983). Figure 9-1 shows the academic segments of the model with the sub components added.

The positive academic integration construct, academic integration, has the following four elements:

- Deep approach is the approach to study adopted by those who seek the underlying meaning of what they read and actively relate it to their own experience and needs.

- Intrinsic motivation is manifest by those who are interested in their subject for its own sake.

- Positive course evaluation means that there has been positive student feedback on course materials, tutoring, assignment marking and administration.

- Reading habit examines the extent to which students enjoy reading and read widely.

Figure 9-1: The Positive and Negative Academic Integration Components

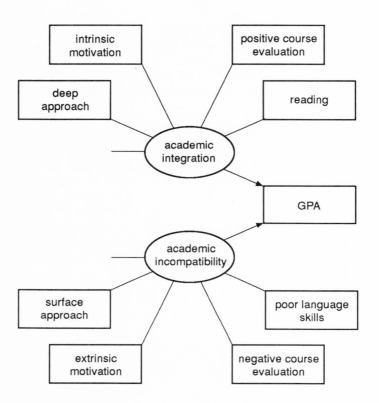

The negative academic integration scale, labeled academic incompatibility, is made up of the following sub-scales:

- Surface approach is the approach adopted by students who focus on the surface aspects of a text. They tend to concentrate on trying to rote-learn factual details which they presume will be relevant to examination questions.

- Extrinsic motivation is that provided by rewards external to the course such as increased promotion opportunities or pay rises if a course is passed.

- Negative course evaluation also examines course materials, tutoring, assignment marking and administration, but this time the student feedback is more negative.

- Language ability is a measure of the students' ability in the language of instruction.

Approaches to Learning

Approaches to learning are direct descriptions of learning processes used by students. The categories used to describe approaches to learning were derived from interviews and observation of students performing normal learning tasks such as reading academic articles.

Marton and Säljö (1976a) identified two discrete approaches to reading articles. Students who used a surface approach concentrated on surface features of the learning task, such as key words or phrases. Their intention was to memorize and reproduce elements which seemed appropriate. When asked about the content of an article, they tended to give detail from examples but had often not grasped the principle of the article.

Students adopting a deep approach concentrate on the underlying meaning of an article. The intention is to understand the real message of a piece of writing or the underlying purpose of an academic task.

Learning approaches have a motivation and a strategy element which are intimately related. Students attempt to understand a topic if it is of real interest to them or if they can see its relevance to their current or future professional roles. On the other hand, a surface approach is associated with limited interest in a task or an extrinsic motivation. In a service course which seems to have little relevance to their main discipline, for example, students might adopt a surface approach and aim to remember the bare essentials to scrape a pass.

The example suggests, as is the case, that learning approaches are not stable psychological traits as are learning styles. Instead the approach adopted depends upon the students' motivation and the prevailing teaching context. Variables such as extrinsic motivation or lack of interest (Fransson, 1977), reproductive assessment questions (Entwistle & Ramsden, 1983, ch. 8; Thomas & Bain, 1984), formal teaching (Ramsden & Entwistle, 1981), a focus on transmitting information (Gow & Kember, 1993; Kember & Gow, 1994), or excessively heavy workload (Dahlgren, 1978;

1984) have all been shown to make the adoption of a surface approach more likely.

To return to the above example, it is, therefore, quite possible that the student who uses a surface approach in the service course might well use a deep approach for learning tasks in another more relevant, better taught course. Laurillard (1984) and Ramsden (1984) include quotations showing students shifting between deep and surface approaches depending on the task and the subject they are taking at the time.

A useful summary of the contrasting characteristics of deep and surface approaches to learning is given by Biggs (1987, p. 15):

> A student who adopts a deep approach:
>
> - is interested in the academic task and derives enjoyment from carrying it out;
> - searches for the meaning inherent in the task (if a prose passage, the intention of the author);
> - personalizes the task, making it meaningful to own experience and to the real world;
> - integrates aspects or parts of task into a whole (for instance, relates evidence to a conclusion), sees relationships between this whole and previous knowledge; and
> - tries to theorize about the task, forms hypothesis.
>
> And, a student who adopts a surface approach:
>
> - sees the task as a demand to be met, a necessary imposition if some other goal is to be reached (a qualification for instance);
> - sees the aspects or parts of the task as discrete and unrelated either to each other or to other tasks;
> - is worried about the time the task is taking;
> - avoids personal or other meanings the task may have; and
> - relies on memorization, attempting to reproduce the surface aspects of the task (the words used, for example, or a diagram or mnemonic).

Learning Approach and Persistence

A distance education study that could be construed as relating to the normative congruence aspect of Tinto's model is that by Kember and Harper (1987). They examined the relationship between attrition and performance and the sixteen sub-scales of the ASI (Ramsden & Entwistle, 1981). It was discovered that the sub-scale which most strongly discriminated between persisters and non-persisters was surface approach.

Students can employ a surface approach or rote learning because it is their habitual study approach or because that type of learning is favored or demanded by the course. Students who habitually employ a surface approach can therefore be seen as having dropped-out because their normal approach to study was not congruent with course demands for a deep-level approach. On the other hand, some students may have dropped-out because they found the surface demands of some courses incompatible with their aspirations for more challenging deeper demands.

Surface Approach

Students who adopt a surface approach direct their attention to the text itself and inevitably employ a reproductive orientation, attempting to memorize facts for subsequent recall in assessment.

> I do all the questions/activities suggested in the study booklets. I try to remember the answers by heart without writing anything down on paper. (Hong Kong–Textiles)

> When reading the course materials or textbooks, I will read them many times until I can remember them by heart. I do not make any notes. I only highlight those theories which might be asked in the examination questions. I memorize those highlighted words for the examination. Once the exam is over, I don't think I can recall those theories. But for tax computation it is different, I still can remember how to do it well because it is also used in my daily job. (Hong Kong–Taxation)

The second of the above quotations indicates the task specific nature of the approach adopted. For study tasks which appeared to have little relevance outside the course the student clearly adopted a surface approach. Ironically the extracts the student deliberately starts out to memorize for the examination are soon forgotten. Where material appears relevant for the student's job a deep approach is adopted and it is this information which is remembered in the long run.

Deep Approach

Students who adopt a deep approach concentrate on the meaning underlying a text because they see its relevance to their needs and find it of interest.

> I use a 'mind map'; that is, I take the key words and link them together or use arrows to show the appropriate direction.... I don't like to memorize; I want to understand the theory. (Hong Kong– Student Guidance)

There is a strong affinity between the deep/surface dichotomy of learning approaches and the underlying assumptions of the distinction between andragogy and pedagogy central to adult learning theory (Knowles, 1970; 1984). Andragogy recognizes the student as capable of at least an element of self-direction and, through experience, of being capable of determining learning needs. Pedagogy places responsibility for determining course content in the hands of the teacher and then expects the student to acquire the defined knowledge. The two constructs are not the same, but andragogical assumptions are more likely to lead to a deep approach while pedagogy will tend to be associated with a surface approach.

Motivation

A great deal has been written on the broad subject of motivation or goal commitment and its relationship to attrition. It seems clear that there is a relationship between the level of the student's goals and persistence. Summerskill's (1962) review concluded that motivation was a critical variable in the drop-out process, but that it had not been operationalized or partialled out well.

Among the results from studies of full-time students, Spaeth (1970) found that higher expectations for future occupational status correlated with high attainment, once ability was controlled. Level of educational goals was found by Sewell and Shah (1967) to be a strong influence on college completion. Trent and Medsker (1968) claimed that persistence was related to the importance students attached to being in college. However, there does appear to be an element of tautology in such a claim, which is clearly a danger in any attempt to link attrition to the students' determination to stay in a program.

However, Knoell (1966) argued that unrealistic goals can be more likely to lead to drop-out than an absence of goals, particularly for those with little intrinsic interest. Abel (1966) found highest drop-out rates among students with clear vocational goals that were unrealistic in terms of their academic ability. Kearney (1969) interviewed Papua New Guinean students to discover their vocational goals. She discovered that there was a significant difference in performance between students identified as being in the wrong institution for their vocational aspirations and those placed in four other categories.

This research on full-time students undoubtedly has a parallel in distance education, though it is not well documented. Students have varying degrees of motivation towards the completion of programs. Most students probably intend to complete a degree but others have clear intentions not to complete one. Students are known to enroll in distance education programs intending to do only a few subjects or units rather than complete a degree. Once enrolled in a full program, however, a student inevitably becomes part of the drop-out statistics even though there was never any intention to complete the program.

In the model intrinsic and extrinsic motivational components appear. Intrinsic motivation refers to the interest students have in the subject matter for its own sake. Extrinsic motivation is concerned with the student's commitment to obtaining a qualification. The presence of intrinsic motivation is related to the student's study approach. Ramsden and Entwistle (1981) found that intrinsic motivation appeared in the same factor as a deep approach. Extrinsic motivation appeared more closely linked with a surface approach. It is, therefore, not surprising that intrinsic motivation is part of the academic integration component, while extrinsic motivation appears in the academic incompatibility component.

Whether students have intrinsic or extrinsic motivation, and the levels of each, will clearly be influenced by the student's characteristics. Extrinsic motivation arises primarily from incentives to obtain a qualification. These are enhanced by situations such as career opportunities barred by lack of qualifications, promotion and financial rewards on course completion, family rivalries to obtain qualifications, or students being of a suitable age to benefit from extra qualifications.

A student's intrinsic motivation is the level of interest in the subject matter itself or interest in learning for its own sake. Intrinsic motivation has an attitudinal aspect and also influences and is influenced by the course evaluation facet of the academic integration component. If the subject matter gels with the student's interests and career needs, then intrinsic motivation will be heightened.

Extrinsic Motivation

Extrinsic motivation is related to the rewards a student might receive by obtaining the degree or other award. The value of a degree to a particular student will be influenced by the student's characteristics. Many of these will be career oriented, such as promotion, salary increases or increased opportunities to find more attractive employment. The home and family situation, the level of existing qualifications, and the student's age will all influence both the additional rewards which would accrue from obtaining the qualification and the need for those rewards.

> Mr P. has a degree already. He withdrew for a variety of reasons. As he was undertaking a part-time management course concurrently with his Open University studies, the two combined proved too great a workload. Furthermore, promotion and long-term staff shortages at work interfered with his studies. (Case B, Kennedy & Powell, 1976, p. 71)

> The course has a lot to offer...if I complete the course I will get a promotion. I would like to go on to do a degree. If I manage the first year part-time I can be sponsored as a full-time student. (PNG student)

The two quotations contrast the effect of extrinsic motivation. The Open University student already had a degree so a further (presumably) bachelors degree would be unlikely to lead to significant additional benefits. In making a cost/benefit decision he chose to continue the management course rather than the OU degree, presumably because the former would be of more benefit. In his case promotion appeared to be a conflicting demand in completing his course rather than a reward which would benefit him if the course were completed.

On the other hand, the Papua New Guinean student could visualize distinct benefits from completing his Matriculation Studies course. He was clearly aiming to go on to do a degree, the sponsorship for the final part of which would be on full pay. Once the degree was acquired there would be opportunities for very rapid advancement.

Students who are extrinsically motivated probably enrolled for the qualification rather than out of interest in the subject matter. Their work and reading are therefore defined by the course prescription and the assessment. As these students may not have any particular interest in the prescribed reading matter, they are more likely to adopt a surface approach and attempt to memorize facts which appear important in the hope that they can be used to answer examination questions.

Intrinsic Motivation

Intrinsic motivation is concerned with the student's interest in the subject matter or content. Deci (1975) found empirical support for the primacy of intrinsic motivation. It may be particularly important for adult students. Knowles (1983) advocates that adult learners be viewed as unique individuals able to determine the relevance of subject matter and skills. Interest in the subject matter for its own sake induces students to search for meaning.

In the case of Open University student B, lack of intrinsic motivation was thought by the counselor to have contributed to the decision to drop-out.

> Finally, as the course was his third choice, he was not as interested in it as he might have been. (Case B, Kennedy & Powell, 1976, p. 71)

The relevance of the course to students' interests and careers affects intrinsic motivation as the following two quotes show.

> I felt History or Geography were two very poor electives for a business studies course. I could not see the relevance, could not get interested in the unit. (University of Tasmania)

> Course is not designed for practical farmers as was indicated in advertisements, etc. (University of Tasmania)

The quotation below is from a student who has intrinsic interest in most of the courses but not in sewing. Unfortunately the course did not offer options.

> So far I enjoy reading the new materials that I haven't touched before, except some boring topics such as Sewing. (Hong Kong–Textiles)

Language

The next sub-components to be considered are concerned with language ability and enthusiasm for reading. The academic incompatibility scale contains the language sub-component, indicating students who do not have a strong command of the language of instruction. The academic integration component contains the reading habit sub-component indicative of enthusiasm for reading and greater language proficiency.

The language sub-component gives an indication that the student is less confident and capable of using the language of instruction. In the DESP inventory higher scores on the sub-scale indicate poorer self-ratings in language ability and lower examination results for the language of instruction. The quotation below is indicative of a student with limited language ability. Any student who has to think so consciously about deciphering the language of the text will find it hard to discern the meaning behind the reading. Such students are operating at sentence or even word level rather than examining a coherent passage.

> To understand a sentence, I will first look at the noun and the verb, then I will be able to catch what the whole sentence roughly means. I underline some key words. Sometimes I will use more simple language to summarize the lengthy sentences. I will draw a table for any area that needs comparison. When I do revision later, I will only refer to the notes that I have made. I try to remember some useful points as well. (Hong Kong–Student Guidance)

Most of the students in the Hong Kong project were studying in a second language, a phenomenon which is common in many other parts of the world. Of the two quotations below, the first is from a student who was confident of English ability. The second quotation indicates a common strategy which some of these second language students adopt. As they lack confidence in their ability to read English fluently they mentally translate into

Chinese as they read, so that they can process and try to understand the content in Chinese. Clearly this makes the study process more difficult.

> I have no problem with the course in English. One thing I appreciate very much is that the author has presented the materials using simple English which is easy to understand. The presentation of materials in English is somehow better than in Chinese. (Hong Kong–Textiles)

> Sometimes I also mentally translate the course materials into Chinese when I read them. (Hong Kong–Textiles)

The reading habit sub-component identifies students who express enthusiasm for reading and claim to read widely and extensively. Enthusiasm for reading also indicates an element of congruence with being a distance education student, since the mode of study involves extensive reading.

> The study materials are not enough. I need to find other reference books to equip myself better. (Hong Kong–Textiles)

Course Evaluations

The academic environment is taken to include all facets of the offering of the course of study by the institution. Included would be the study package mailed to the student, mediated lessons (via video or computer conferences etc.), the interaction via assignments, any tutorial assistance provided, and any other interactions between student and institution of either an academic or administrative nature.

When considering the study package, the student is mainly in need of normative congruence. There are questions as to whether the content and curriculum design are compatible with the student's perceived career needs and interests. There should be congruence between the student's approach to study and the instructional design of the course of study. Ideally the media mix employed should suit the learning style of the students.

There is also the possibility of introducing an element of affiliation towards the institution by the use of an interactive and personal style by the course writer. Collective affiliation is also established through the interactions associated with academic support for the courses. Such variables as the frequency and nature of contacts, the speed of response to student initiated contacts, the provision of local tutorials or the use of telephone or satellite conferencing can all contribute to whether or not the student has any positive feelings of association with the institution.

Collective affiliation could also be influenced by administrative support or the lack of it. The student who meets no administrative snags and has queries answered promptly and accurately could build an impression of dealing with a competent professional organization with which the student feels happy to be associated. On the other hand, students who encounter overpowering bureaucratic requirements, administrative incompetence or slow responses to queries could rapidly build up a sense of disenchantment and even hostility towards the organization.

Both of the components dealing with academic integration have sub-components addressing course evaluation issues. The academic integration component has a positive course evaluation sub-component, while the corresponding sub-component in academic incompatibility is called negative course evaluation.

Negative Course Evaluation

The sub-component negative course evaluation indicates students expressing dissatisfaction with the course and its support. Either these are inadequate for the student's needs or the student is incompatible with the mode of course offering. Either way there is a lack of normative congruence in Durkheim's (1961) terms. The four quotations below show four aspects of the negative impression of the course sub-scale: the course materials, the tutoring, assignment marking and course administration respectively:

> I don't find the course interesting because I know most of the basic ideas about clothing and textiles.... For me, the course is dull and lengthy. (Hong Kong–Textiles)

> There are a few irresponsible tutors too. For instance, one tutor asked the class whether anyone in the class had any problem or not, otherwise the class was dismissed. It is really a waste, not only of our time, but also our money. (Hong Kong–Textiles)

Some tutors are terrible, the comments made are just 'Try your best'; that is all for the tutor's comment. Some of the bad comments are as follows: 'You have answered four options but you still owe two more options.' The tutor didn't give the answers for the two options. I was not too sure that I finally found the answers from the book. I wouldn't have missed those two options if I had known them beforehand. Can I suggest that model answers be provided? (Hong Kong–Textiles)

...once where the mailing of the tutorial time table was sent to the wrong address. This caused me to fail to attend the first tutorial class where I should have been able to pick up my first batch of course materials. The tutor concerned was rude to me when I phoned him to explain my situation. Most of the marked assignments are returned late, especially this term. (Hong Kong–Textiles)

Positive Course Evaluation

The positive course evaluation sub-component deals with the same areas of a course, but this time the students give more positive feedback. The quotations below address the same four elements of the course as in the above quotations for the negative evaluation. This time they are referred to in positive ways. As before the quotations below refer to (in order); course materials, tutoring, assignment marking and administration.

I am impressed by the author who gave some activities to be worked out after each chapter. It is preferable that the theme/main ideas/main points of the chapter are shown through the activities. (Hong Kong–Textiles)

There are two tutors who are performing their job excellently. They explain the materials in precise ways, show us which sections are relevant to daily work and how to put them into practice in our job, what units to pay attention to; all these are what actually I expect from the tutors. (Hong Kong–Textiles)

The comments on returned assignment are helpful because I am reminded by the tutor about my weak areas in answering questions. For instance I will be told that certain questions should be answered in more specific and precise format. Therefore I won't make the same mistake again during the examination. (Hong Kong–Textiles)

The course was administered well. The whole package of study
materials was delivered at one time before the course began. The
model answers for the assignments were sent to me promptly and
the instructions were clear to me. (Hong Kong–Textiles)

It is interesting to note that students can have such different
assessments of the same courses or that the same students can
have quite different reactions to different subjects within a course.
In part, these differing reactions are due to encountering different
tutors and having contrasting experiences with the administrative
staff. Part of the divergence, in course evaluations, also seems
likely to be a function of whether the students' background
enables them to integrate with the expectations of the course and
the requirements of each of its facets.

In Durkheim's terms (1961), whether students give positive or
negative ratings to course evaluations can be interpreted as
indicating the congruence between course and student and also
revealing the extent to which collective affiliation had developed.
As the evaluated components of a course are normally those most
amenable to action from the college it is worth examining the
various evaluated facets of courses from the perspective of
collective affiliation and normative congruence.

Collective Affiliation

The essence of the collective affiliation side of academic
integration is the quality and quantity of contact between the
student and the organization. The personal contact of tutorials
seems to be particularly effective at providing collective
affiliation.

When I know a tutor is coming for a visit I work hard to catch up
with the assignments. I can ask the tutor about all the work I did
not understand. After the visits I always feel encouraged so I work
hard. (PNG student)

A detailed diagnosis was sent to the Senior Counselor who
authorized special sessions. Dr S., Dr P. and I (the counselor also
did some tutoring in science) have all agreed to mark late work
with the concurrence of the senior counselor and the staff tutor.

This student is generally weak. He is also taking two courses. I
think he would have struggled in any case without his long

working hours. However if he makes it at the end of the year, our efforts will have been worthwhile.

(Mr L. is still studying with the Open University in 1976, even though in 1974 he was made redundant at work.) (Case A, Kennedy & Powell, 1976, p. 71)

In both quotations it is apparent that the actions of the tutors are making a significant contribution to the student's collective affiliation. In the case of Mr L., even the brief counseling notes convey the efforts of the tutors and the relationship which would have built up between counselor and student. These supportive actions must have established a high degree of integration between student and the academic institution. The integration would have strengthened the student's commitment in subsequent passes through the cycle in the model.

Direct personal contact is undoubtedly highly beneficial towards building up collective affiliation. It also appears to be possible to develop collective affiliation through telephone contact and presumably by mail.

Before the telephone tutorials were introduced I was studying in complete isolation. I had no contact with other students and the only contact with lecturers was the comments on assignments. I think the telephone tutorials are a good idea because Philosophy is a difficult subject to study by yourself. (University of Tasmania)

Negative reactions to academic staff can mean that integration does not occur. Another student cited as a contributing reason for his withdrawal:

...the arrogant manner of the lecturer-in-charge in his consideration of late assignments and his decision in failing my work. (University of Tasmania)

Of the evidence gathered in case studies the vast majority indicated the positive integrative role of tutors. However the following quotation shows that not all students appreciate the efforts of tutors to enhance collective affiliation.

The tutors I had dealings with were a little too demanding in that they more or less insisted on tutorial participation which I thought was voluntary. The continual amount of phone calls, especially in the 1st semester, from my computing tutor turned me off the course to begin with as I undertook the course with the intent of achieving

> a result without someone standing over me watching my every
> step. (University of Tasmania)

Students who wish to be totally independent learners would
obviously prefer tutorials or residential schools to be optional.

Administrative support services, as well as academic, can also
play a part in either enhancing or curtailing collective affiliation.
Unfortunate experiences can create lasting impressions with
individuals, even if the remaining service has been very good.
Contrasting views of the same service can result.

> Need more prompt deliveries of assignments and more direct
> feedback. Assignments are always late back and the University
> doubles up on just about all it's mail–I receive 2 or more copies of
> some study items and no copies of other ones. Maybe admin needs
> drastic reorganizing. (University of Tasmania)

> In my case, I can find nothing to suggest, at this stage, which could
> improve the already excellent service, advice and encouragement I
> have received from the External Studies Unit to date. Due to
> changes in my personal business work load, I find I am currently
> unable to devote enough study time to complete this unit, however,
> I look forward to further contact as an external student in the new
> year and would like to express my thanks to all the people involved
> in the External Studies Unit for their cheerful and friendly help and
> advice in the past. (University of Tasmania)

Normative Congruence

The other element of integration in Durkheim's (1961) model of
suicide is that of value integration or normative congruence.
When translated into a model of drop-out from distance
education, the component of academic integration will include
issues like whether there is congruence between the curriculum
and the student's interests and career needs. The instructional
design needs to gel with the approach to study of the students
and the media package should be congruent with the learning
style of the students.

The academic integration component of the model will often be
strongly influenced by the educational background facet of the
characteristics component. Those with limited exposure to the
educational system will find it more difficult to integrate with the

norms of academic study. Their ability to make necessary adjustments will be influenced by their goal commitment.

> Mr X. Aged 48. This student stopped submitting work and did not go to Summer School on medical advice.

> He regularly attended the study centre in the early weeks of the course. A great deal of time was given to him by another counselor and myself because it was obvious that he had no idea of using Social Science concepts and yet was extremely convinced of his knowledge and ability.

> Poor grades and a warning from the tutor led to more intensive efforts to help him. These were hindered by a change of job which made him unable to come to the study centre. Offers of special sessions were turned down as Mr H. was convinced that the next TMA was going to be a good one ...he stopped submitting work because of illness (he had a heart attack last year), but the low assignment grades were a contributory factor in his withdrawal.

> There were certain psychological problems–could not stop talking– saw everything in terms of himself (this is related to the poverty of the essays).

> Left school at 14 but claimed to be widely read. Written English is quite good but he is incapable of using the study material as a basis for his essay. The problems set seem to him so obvious that they can be answered in a few words. But, above all, he sees all the problems in terms of his own experience. (Case D, Kennedy & Powell, 1976, p. 72)

A major reason for withdrawal in this case seems to have been the total inability of the student to integrate with the academic norms of the University. The approach to problems, in which answers were briefly given in terms of the student's own experiences, is totally at odds with the accepted value system of academic study.

Academic study is rather like a game with rules, conventions and codes of behavior. To be successful a student has to learn the rules and integrate behavior with the accepted norms. Leaving school early has deprived the student of exposure to academic conventions and clearly the tutors were unable to remedy the initial handicap. Constant rebuttals in the form of low grades for work, which the student thought was good, would clearly lower the perceived benefits of continuing with the course.

The two quotations below are from students who have had problems adjusting their conceptions of knowledge to that required for college study. In Perry's (1988) terms both students appear to have started from a position of basic duality, believing that there are definitive right answers to all problems. For their courses they have had to move towards a more relativistic position recognizing multiple viewpoints. Both students realized that their conception of academe was not in line with course expectations so they did appreciate that change is necessary, even if that was a hard process. If the students do not realize that there is incompatibility, as seemed to be the case with Mr X above, then change cannot even start.

> There are a lot of study materials sent to us and they are difficult to understand. The learning style is different from the conventional style, the present learning demands a lot of independent thinking in which I am short. It is hard for me to get out from the previous conventional learning, thus means my course grade is not that good! (Hong Kong–OLIHK)

> In the beginning of the course, I am not getting used to the Australian's learning style since I have been adapted to the learning style in Hong Kong. Free thinking is in fact the aim of the course. I now realize that there is no definite solution to the task. (Hong Kong–Education)

The problem experienced by the above student was quite common to others in the course, which was designed to promote critical inquiry. For the student below, collective affiliation helped to overcome the normative congruence predicament. This is an interesting case of the interaction of the two aspects of integration. Well developed collective affiliation remedied an instance of normative incongruence.

> Yes, I felt discouraged and frustrated and often came close to giving up when I worked on my first assignment. Luckily the support from my group kept me in the course. I knew that I wasn't the only person to have problems with the first assignment, there were the same problems faced by my group mates as well. Now, I do not have the feeling of giving up since I understand its learning approach–free thinking. (Hong Kong–Education)

Summary

As this has been a longish chapter, it is worth repeating the conceptual diagram given in the synopsis at the start of the chapter. The two positive and negative academic integration components each have four sub-components of the type shown in Figure 9-2.

Figure 9-2: Sub-components of the Academic Integration Scales

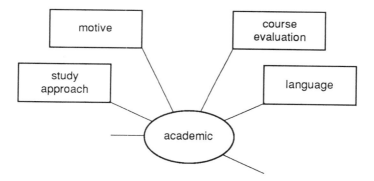

Both positive and negative academic integration scales have sub-components for an approach to learning. Academic integration has deep approach while academic incompatibility has surface approach. The motivation sub-components are intrinsic motivation for the positive track and extrinsic motivation for the negative. The course evaluation sub-components are simply labeled positive and negative respectively. The final sub-components refer to language and reading ability. For the positive track the sub-component refers to students expressing enjoyment from reading. The sub-component for the negative track gives an indication as to whether a student's language ability equips them for courses which normally rely heavily on reading.

Two further concepts which have been important in this chapter are the two elements of integration form Durkheim's model (1961), namely collective affiliation and normative congruence. These are not specifically shown on the conceptual diagram because they apply generally across the academic and social integration components.

Students with limited educational experience are likely to find difficulty in achieving normative congruence with the demands and conventions of academe. They might find that their conceptions of academic study are inconsistent with those of the faculty. Even more experienced students can find particular courses incompatible with their expectations and aspirations.

Collective affiliation between the student and faculty and/or institution or among groups of students can have a very positive influence on student progress. Collective affiliation is likely to develop through positive experiences of personal contact, though such contact can also damage relationships if the students are disenchanted with the nature of the experience.

Chapter 10

Course Completion or Drop-out?

Synopsis

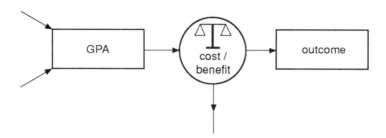

The model incorporates a cost/benefit analysis. The student has to decide whether the opportunity costs of time spent studying are worthwhile in terms of interest in the subject matter, benefits from the eventual qualification or other rewards the student might derive from study.

Changes to variables in the model will affect the nature of the cost benefit decision. The model accommodates for these changes by a recycling loop. Students in changeable situations or at risk of dropping-out are likely to re-assess their cost/benefit situation frequently.

Following the discussion in Chapter 2, it is important to carefully define measures of progress or drop-out. Two measures were used in the quantitative studies. Grade Point Average (GPA) provided a measure of academic achievement. The main measure of persistence was the ratio of modules or subjects completed to those attempted.

Cost/Benefit Analysis

The final component of the model, before a decision to drop-out or continue, is a cost/benefit analysis by the student. The student has to decide whether the opportunity costs of time spent studying are worthwhile in view of the perceived benefits of the eventual qualification, the interest in the course, or other benefits the student might derive from studying.

In this analysis the student weighs the benefits of continuing the course of study against the costs accrued. The benefits would include any material and status benefits which would result from completing the course and enjoyment the student would gain from intrinsic interest in the subject matter. There may also be pleasure in participating in any local tutorials or study schools. Against these potential benefits the student has to weigh costs which are both financial and non-financial. The financial costs include fees, textbooks, travel to any tutorials or residential schools, and possibly loss of earning opportunities. Often the non-financial costs will be more significant. They arise because the time spent studying means that the student has less time to spend on family and social activities.

In the cost/benefit analysis the student essentially confronts the type of reasons reported for dropping-out in autopsy studies and discussed at length in Chapter 8, which deals with the way students who drop-out attribute the cause to external factors. The most commonly reported reason is "insufficient time for study." In arriving at the decision to withdraw, the student must have decided that time spent studying yielded insufficient benefit compared to the advantages which accrued from allocating time to work, family, or social activities.

The two quotations below provide contrasting illustrations of the cost/benefit analysis step, interpreted in terms of the allocation of time. This first student faces this cost/benefit analysis frequently. The student appears to derive greater benefit from going out with friends, a process which if continually adopted must lead to failure or drop-out. The cost of social scorn outweighs the longer term benefits which might accrue from spending more time studying. For the second student the benefits form the course are sufficient to outweigh the cost of giving up the football games.

> I can't reject my friends' invitation to go out as it is rather difficult
> and childish if I give them the reason that I can't go out because I
> have to study at home. (Hong Kong–OLIHK)

> I have to sacrifice my football time on Sunday mornings because
> that is now becoming the tutorial time. (Hong Kong–OLIHK)

Similar explanations apply to students who blame their
withdrawal on external events such as job transfers or illnesses.
They have perceived that, in the light of their changed
circumstances, the costs of continuing with their course are now
greater than the perceived benefits.

Changes to the Cost/Benefit Equation

The variables incorporated in the model will not normally remain
constant during a student's academic career. Background
characteristics will alter as the, often quite lengthy, program
proceeds. Motivation will vary during this time, often being
strengthened towards the end as completion comes into view.
Intrinsic interest will differ from module to module. The degree
of both academic and social integration will be influenced by
changes in characteristics, development of goal commitment, the
nature of courses, support from the institution, and events and
attitudes in the work, family, and social environments. These
changes to the variables in the model will affect the nature of the
cost/benefit decision.

The quotation below illustrates a change in the cost/benefit
equation. Once the heavy alternative demands of the first
semester have passed, the balance tilts in favor of continued
study.

> I find it difficult to follow the study schedule. As school work keeps
> me busy all the time during school days, I find that the time for
> taking rest during the school holiday is also discarded now because
> I am forced to read the course materials. I have often thought of
> giving up in the first term. We used to be very busy during the
> months of September to December when we have to do a lot of
> preparations for the public exam sitters such as Form 5 and Form 7.
> The work pressure is high for me. They will go for the public exam
> in April/May and thereafter they won't be back to school again.
> Now I feel relaxed in the second term and I am in a good mood as

well. My intention of giving this course up disappeared. (Hong Kong–Student Guidance)

Having passed through the initial crisis, the balance has swung markedly in favor of continuing the course. This student is unlikely to examine the cost/benefit status now unless there is some marked further change to the other variables in the system. The student making the quotation below is in quite a different situation. In this case the cost/benefit analysis will be made often.

> I do not have any confidence to be a successful distance learning student. I always think of giving it up. Time constraints, boring courses, such as sewing, are the factors that influence me much. (Hong Kong–Textiles)

Students will reassess the relative benefits of continuing study as the course proceeds. For students who are at danger, because they have not integrated academic demands with their lifestyle, the reassessment will be frequent, as they weigh the counter attractions to picking up their study booklets. Students who have achieved academic and social integration may only reassess the benefits after some major change in circumstances affects one or more of the components of the model. The goal of completing the course will be fixed in their minds and their lifestyle will have adapted to permit a schedule of study. The further students progress into a course the greater the cost of not completing it. The hours of study and the sacrifices already made would all go to waste if a course is abandoned in the latter stages. Course fees paid for the initial stages will also be perceived as a financial outlay with no return.

> Yes, I did feel discouraged when I knew I would have to spend at least 6 years to complete the whole study and there were expensive school fees I had to pay each year. I wondered whether it was worthwhile to study due to the long study periods and the expensive school fees. Now I no longer come close to giving it up because so far I have invested so much money in it and it is really a waste if I drop out from study now. (Hong Kong–OLIHK)

Recycling Loop

The model allows for the changing nature of variables by including a recycling loop. The loop returns to the entry characteristics component, the starting point of the model.

Returning to this point allows for the incorporation of any alterations to these background variables, such as changes in employment or family circumstances, or enhanced levels of educational preparedness. For some students the entry characteristics will not have changed—the recycling would have been precipitated by modifications to one or more of the integration components. In these cases the students can be envisaged as passing through the entry characteristics component with zero change status, which is more convenient than altering the point at which the loop returns.

The examples given for each component have shown how each component can be influenced by preceding components in the model. These examples will also have illustrated the dynamic nature of the variables within components.

Each time major changes occur within the variable set for a component, the student can be envisaged as progressing through the components of the model to confront the cost/benefit analysis. As explained in the previous section, the frequency of passes through the model can be seen to depend on the stability of the student's characteristics and the strength of their commitment. During a course a student will pass through the loop a number of times. Each time some variables will be different and each time the student will encounter the cost/benefit analysis.

Following are two case studies which show the operation of the cost/benefit analysis step in conjunction with the recycling loop. In the first, cost is literally a financial cost. Note, though, that the support from the employer would go well beyond that of enabling the student to afford to attend residential school. It would have a marked impact on social integration by sending a clear message that the course was seen as important. The student has clearly changed from the negative to the positive track.

> At a recent residential school a student told me he was about to drop-out shortly after receiving his autumn session materials. Although over two-thirds of the way to finishing a degree the financial cost of being a student was becoming too much. He was required to attend another residential school in May which for him meant an amount of around $300 for accommodation and travel costs. He reached the stage where expenses (costs) outweighed benefits and he was not prepared to continue what to him appeared to be a selfish use of the limited money available to his family. His

goal commitment dissipated and he decided sadly to write and inform the University of his decision to withdraw. Fortunately for this student, a new boss arrived in his office at about this time who was particularly impressed to see he had already completed two-thirds of a degree. Aware of the benefits that might accrue to the business if the degree was completed and the employee realized an ambition, the boss offered to pay all the remaining residential school costs. Here was enormously encouraging support from the workplace which consequently rekindled the student's goal commitment. The scales tipped back in favor of the benefits and the withdrawal letter was never sent. (Roberts, Boyton, Buete & Dawson, 1991, p. 59)

The next case study contains answers to a series of questions by one student. This time, as is undoubtedly much more common, the costs and benefits are not posed in financial terms. Instead the costs are those of opportunity. When the student faces both a demanding assessment schedule and a busy time at work, then time cost is high and some social options must be foregone if the course is to be continued. The student is particularly at risk at this time because of the low state of academic integration following the long break since past study activity. Success in those initial assignments leads to growing confidence and academic integration is heightened. As work demands recede the alternative costs are reduced and the next cycle is along the positive track.

> In fact, I didn't expect to have so many assignments. I only expected one assignment for each subject. Although there is a colloquium for each subject, which carries no continuous assessment mark, but we also have to spend a lot of time in preparing it for presentation. I don't feel happy spending too much time on the assignments.

> At the beginning, I felt very confident, I thought I was able to master all the course materials. Later in November I felt depressed for the heavy workload when the heavy school work and assignments come together. I have not written any essays for nearly ten years. I was afraid that I could not complete them all at one time. However, after that critical period, my confidence has built up again.

> I felt depressed last November when school work had to be completed urgently. I was not able to catch up the time table as suggested in this course. I felt emotional and discouraged from

doing this course during that critical period. At that time, I blamed myself that I would not enroll in this course if I knew it was a very time consuming course. However I felt relaxed now as the school work is not that tight for these months. (Hong Kong–Education)

The presence of the feedback loop provides a mechanism or route for students to switch from the negative to the positive track or vice versa. Students may initially find integration difficult so be best classified along the external attribution and academic incompatibility track. After changes of circumstance, increase in motivation, or efforts by the institution or themselves to achieve better integration it is possible that the students could recycle through the longitudinal model. On this occasion, though, with a new set of starting attributes more attuned to integration they would be on the positive track.

It is of course possible for students to make the opposite switch. Those who seem to have achieved social integration and be compatible with academic expectations can lose motivation or interest in a course or find that their environment changes so as to disturb their equilibrium in their social or academic spheres. Again this category of student will enter a new loop of the model, but this time the student must be seen as one at-risk because the new circumstances indicate movement along the negative track.

The presence of the recycling loop and the possibility of switching tracks is important in both theoretical and practical terms. Without the possibility of switching to another track students become locked onto an inevitable path towards either success or failure. This gives rise to a similar problem to that inherent in research into relationships between entry characteristics and course outcomes. When a causal relationship is posited it implies inexorable progress towards some pre-destined goal regardless of the actions of the student or the institution.

The presence of the re-cycling loop and the possibility of re-entry on the alternative track raises quite different implications. Progress is no longer inevitable but now depends on the efforts and attitude of the student and the actions and environment of the institution. Both parties have an opportunity to influence outcomes and by implication a responsibility to play a part in ensuring that desired outcomes are achieved.

Outcome Measures

The model aims to give insight into both how well students will perform academically and whether or not a course will be completed. The model attempts to examine student progress towards academic success rather than concentrating exclusively on the more negative outcome of drop-out. It therefore needs a measure of academic attainment and another showing the proportion of a course completed. This is accomplished by the inclusion of GPA and the outcome measure of the ratio of enrolled modules completed. Definitions of GPA and outcome ratio, used in the quantitative studies, are given in the next chapter.

The position of GPA in the model requires explanation. The original intention was to treat GPA purely as an outcome variable. The quantitative analysis, though, suggested that GPA functioned to some extent as an intervening variable between academic incompatibility and drop-out. Presumably students who receive low grades, after working through a module or course, tend to be discouraged from continuing with further modules. Students proceeding on the negative track through external attribution and academic incompatibility are likely to attain lower GPA scores and a hence there is a greater likelihood of drop-out. As in the original Tinto model (1975) grades influence decisions on persistence. A student who works hard all semester only to receive a low grade may well decide to take no further modules. On the other hand, a good grade can serve as the stimulus for further study.

Conclusion

The addition of the outcome measures has now completed the development of the model. The provision of the cost/benefit analysis shows how students balance the decision between persistence and drop-out. Those on the positive track may confront the cost/benefit decision quite rarely. Students on the negative track are more likely to have it at the front of their minds.

The inclusion of the recycling loop is important as it provides a mechanism for switching from one track to the other. It allows students to take charge of their own destiny. It means that the college and the faculty can influence students' academic progress and suggests they have a moral obligation to try to influence students towards the positive track.

Having completed the derivation and explanation of the model from diverse qualitative data in Part B, the next step is to test it using quantitative data. Part C presents two discrete tests of the model using data derived from the DESP inventory.

Part C

Quantitative Tests of the Model

Chapter 11

Initial Quantitative Test of the Model

Synopsis

The initial quantitative test of the model involved students enrolled for three programs in Hong Kong. Students in the courses were asked to complete the DESP inventory. First and second order factor analysis was used to form questionnaire items into scales and sub-scales corresponding to the model components described in earlier chapters. These scales were then related to entry characteristics and outcome variables to form the path model. There was a good fit between the quantitative model and the qualitative version developed in Part B.

Triangulation

To suit the sequence and the conceptual development within the book, the contents of this chapter are presented as an initial quantitative test of a model which has been developed and illuminated by qualitative data over the preceding six chapters. In practice the sequence between quantitative and qualitative analysis was not as discrete as has been portrayed within the book. The original published accounts of the initial quantitative test of the model (Kember, Murphy, Siaw & Yuen, 1991; Kember, Lai, Murphy, Siaw & Yuen, 1992a) show that qualitative and quantitative data collection were simultaneous and that the quantitative analysis was as exploratory as the qualitative. Presenting the exploratory side of the quantitative analysis serves no useful purpose at this stage of the book and could cause confusion to its logical development. The analysis is, therefore, shown as if the model had been reasonably well formed before the testing process started, as was the case for the replication test reported in the next chapter.

Sample

The sample for the initial quantitative test was students from three of the programs examined in the Hong Kong study. Information about these programs was given in Chapter 5, and they are among the programs from which qualitative information was drawn for Chapters 6 to 10. The programs examined were those in textiles and clothing, taxation and business administration. The programs ranged in level from Certificate to Masters degree. Further details of the programs and demographic information on the students enrolling in them is contained in Kember, Lai, Murphy, Siaw and Yuen (1992b).

The populations for these programs were approximately 540, 400 and 90 respectively. An attempt was made to treat the entire enrolled population as the sample for the study. The overall response rate for the survey was 61%, which is a high return for distance education courses, and quite sufficient to be seen as representative.

The DESP questionnaire was administered to students about five weeks after the start of each course. The time was chosen as being early enough to obtain responses from students who eventually dropped out, yet late enough for the students to have sufficient experience to respond meaningfully. It was desirable to include in the survey students who would subsequently not complete the course, and this necessitates a reasonably early administration of the inventory since a high proportion of drop-outs from distance education courses tend to occur at an early stage (Kember, 1981; McIntosh, Woodley & Morrison, 1980). The questionnaire was distributed to students either at tutorials or by mail. Follow-up letters were sent to non-respondents after the initial mailing so as to maximize the response rate.

The students were sent a Chinese version of the instrument since almost all use English as a second language. The instrument was developed in English and the items were then translated into Chinese by a team of three translators. Independent back translation was used to check the accuracy of the translation.

Questionnaire

The original version of the questionnaire was longer than that given in Appendix B as the work was still somewhat exploratory. The instrument then contained additional items that the research team thought might relate in some way to student persistence. This chapter refers only to items which emerged from the exploratory factor analysis in factors which were conceptually plausible.

The questionnaire starts with items relating to enrollment characteristics—the type of demographic information often sought at the start of a course. The remainder of the questionnaire consists of items forming the sub-scales for each of the components of the model. For these items students were asked to respond on a five point Likert scale from definitely agree to definitely disagree.

Items forming the sub-scales will be described component by component in the order in which they have been described in Part B. The component in the positive track will be dealt with before the corresponding one from the negative track. The full questionnaire is given in Appendix B.

Background Characteristics

The questionnaire inquired about a range of demographic information so as to build a profile of typical Hong Kong students (Kember, Lai, Murphy, Siaw & Yuen, 1992b). The information which was subsequently used in the model is as below.

Sex (1=male; 2=female)

Age

Years of working experience

Salary

Marital status (1=married; 2=single)

Highest academic qualification (from 1=not completed Form 5 to 6=university degree)

Social Integration

In the questionnaire the social integration component is made up of three sub-scales.

Enrollment encouragement (3 items)

> Sample item: My employer encouraged me to enroll in this course.

Study encouragement (2 items)

> Sample item: My family encouraged me to study because they thought the qualification was important.

Family support (2 items).

> Sample item: I usually spend a lot of time with family.

External Attribution

Insufficient time (4 items)

> Sample item: As I work long hours it is difficult to find time to study.

Events hinder study (2 items)

> Sample item: Personal/family circumstances, unseen at the time of enrollment, hindered my studies.

Distractions (5 items)

> Sample item: My spouse became annoyed because I spent so much time studying.

Potential drop-out (2 items).

> Sample item: I often wonder whether all the study is worth the effort.

Academic Integration

The positive and negative academic integration scales have corresponding components. Each contains a sub-scale measuring: approach to study, motivation, impression of the course, and language usage. In both cases the approach to study and motivation sub-scales are adapted from the Approaches to Studying Inventory (ASI) (Entwistle & Ramsden, 1983).

The positive academic integration scale has the following sub-scales.

Deep approach (4 items)

> Sample item: I usually set out to understand thoroughly the meaning of what I am asked to read.

Intrinsic motivation (4 items)

> Sample item: I find that studying academic topics can often be really exciting.

Positive course evaluation (4 items)

> Sample item: The activities/self-assessment questions have helped me to learn.

Positive telephone counseling (2 items)

> Sample item: The telephone counseling service is useful.

Reading habit (2 items).

> Sample item: I enjoy reading so I am suited to distance learning courses.

Academic Incompatibility

The academic incompatibility scale is made up of the following sub-scales. The potential drop-out sub-scale appears in both the academic incompatibility and the external attribution scale described previously.

Surface approach (6 items)

> Sample item: When I'm reading I try to memorize important facts which may come in useful later.

Extrinsic motivation (4 items)

> Sample item: I chose the present course mainly to give me a chance of a really good job afterwards.

Negative course evaluation (6 items)

> Sample item: The learning materials are presented in a confusing way.

Potential drop-out (2 items).

> Sample item: I often wonder whether all the study is worth the effort.

English ability (4 items)

> Sample item: What grade were you awarded in English Language in the HKCEE examination?

The English language ability sub-scale was formed by combining responses from three self-rating items asking participants to rate their own ability, on five-point scales, in reading, writing and speaking English, together with a score based on a public examination result. The Cronbach alpha of the English ability sub-scale was 0.77. A study making use of the English language ability sub-scale has been reported previously (Gow, Kember & Chow, 1991).

Outcome Variables

Two outcome variables were used in the model. Grade Point Average (GPA) was a score from 0% to 100%, in which 50% was normally regarded as a minimum passing rate. Each program had a modular format so it was possible to use a student's current mean grade as a measure of academic achievement.

The other outcome measure was the ratio of the number of modules failed/number of modules attempted. Scores range from zero, for passing all attempted modules, to one for failing all attempted modules. Scores in the zero to one range indicate the proportion of modules completed. The ratio was used as a measure of student persistence within the program. Most students who dropped-out ceased submitting assignments or did not attend the examination rather than formally withdrawing. They therefore received an official grade of fail, so the ratio measures persistence more than examination failure.

Outcome measures were not obtained from the questionnaire. They were obtained separately from the college in question either at the end of the course or after a cut-off point corresponding to one academic year of study.

The potential drop-out sub-scale was listed in the two scales in the negative track of the model. This sub-scale reveals that the student has been giving consideration to withdrawing. In the qualitative analysis this corresponds to a facet of the cost/benefit analysis. As such the potential drop-out sub-scale gives an indication of potential outcomes.

Reliability of Sub-scales

A reliability test was conducted for the sub-scales derived for the DESP inventory. The Cronbach alpha coefficient for each sub-scale is listed in Table 11-1.

Table 11-1: Reliabilities of DESP Sub-scales

Sub-scale	
Enrollment encouragement	0.69
Study encouragement	0.52
Family support	0.39
Positive course evaluation	0.54
Positive telephone counseling	0.67
Reading habit	0.44
Insufficient time	0.71
Events hinder study	0.61
Distractions	0.54
Potential drop-out	0.50
Negative course evaluation	0.54

Second-order Factor Analysis

Second-order factor analysis was then conducted to examine the way the sub-scales combined into scales. Principal component analysis was used followed by varimax rotation (SPSS Inc., 1986). Table 11-2 gives the resulting five-factor structure. The table omits the decimal points before the factor loadings and gives only loadings of 0.3 or greater.

Table 11-2: Second Order Factor Analysis

Sub-scale / Factor	1	2	3	4	5
Enrollment encouragement	86				
Study encouragement	42				
Family support	62				
Insufficient time			61		
Events hinder study			43		
Distractions			75		
Deep approach		51			
Intrinsic motivation		73			
Reading habit		49			
Positive course evaluation		33			52
Positive telephone counseling		31			33
Surface approach				57	
Extrinsic motivation				33	
English ability				41	
Negative course evaluation				51	
Potential drop-out			31	38	
Eigenvalue	3.26	2.24	1.51	1.36	1.06
% of variance explained	17.1	11.8	7.9	7.1	5.6

The factor analysis is in line with the four scales described above. Factor 1 is social integration, factor 2 is academic integration, factor 3 is external attribution and factor 4 is academic incompatibility. Sub-scales appear in the factor corresponding to the hypothesized main scales. The fifth factor shows that the two positive course evaluation sub-scales exist as co-factors in factors 2 and 5.

Reliability tests were then performed on the four main scales. Table 11-3 shows the Cronbach alpha values.

Table 11-3: Scale Reliabilities

Scale	Reliability
Social integration	0.68
External attribution	0.61
Academic integration	0.65
Academic incompatibility	0.55

Formation of a Model

The factor analysis and the reliability tests confirmed that the DESP inventory contained reasonable measures of the components and sub-components derived from the qualitative data. The next step was an attempt to link the scales together into a path model. The aim was to see whether the quantitative data fitted the conceptual model described in Part B.

Pre-entry or background characteristics should be the starting point of the path model. The four main scales become intervening variables. The model hypothesizes positive and negative paths both containing social and academic integration variables of a contrasting nature. The progress criteria, used to indicate completion or drop-out, are the resulting outcome measures.

Path Analysis

Path analysis is a technique used to test the fit of variables to a hypothesized model. It is an application of multiple regression to a causal model derived from theoretical considerations (Kerlinger & Pedhazur, 1973) and assumes linear, additive and causal relationship among the variables in the model (Duncan, 1966; Land, 1969). Each dependent variable is assumed to be explained by some combination of independent variables in the model, or when it is not possible to explain all variation, then the residual or error terms are taken into account. The residual terms are assumed to be independent and normally distributed (Kim & Kohout, 1975). Fortunately, regression analysis is fairly robust (i.e., unaffected by the violation of assumptions), and therefore the violation of either of the assumptions is permissible to a certain degree (Bean, 1979).

The model in this study is shown in Figure 11-1. It is a recursive model, that is one constructed with a one-way causal flow system (Kerlinger & Pedhazur, 1973). The causal order is read from left to right. Each arrow is called a path and each has a path coefficient obtained from the ordinary least square method of multiple regression. As the variables were standardized, the betas or standardized regression coefficients are comparable. They indicate the direction (either plus or minus) and magnitude of influence between variables. Only significant beta or path coefficients are included in the model. Non-significant paths were eliminated and the regression recomputed with significant variables.

An indication of the fit of the model is given by values for the coefficients of determination (R^2) and error terms or residuals (e). These are given in Table 11-4.

Table 11-4: Residuals and R^2 Values for the Original Model

Scale	R^2	Residual
Social integration	0.10	0.96
External attribution	0.15	0.93
Academic integration	0.18	0.91
Academic incompatibility	0.15	0.93
GPA	0.10	0.95
Ratio	0.80	0.45

Figure 11-1: The Path Model for the Original Test

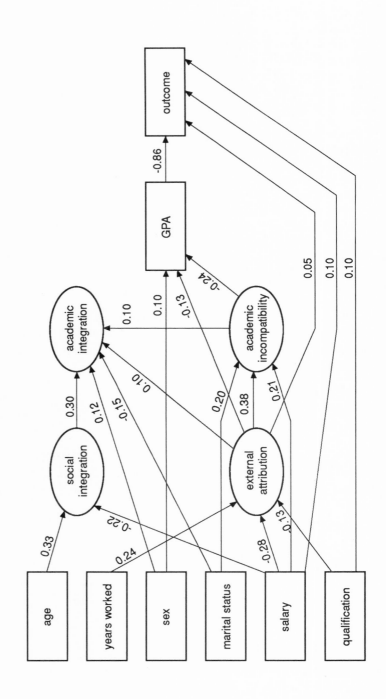

Discussion

The path model shows a good fit with the model described in Part B. Specifically, few of the background variables are significantly related to either of the outcome variables. The three correlations which do exist have, at maximum, the low level of 0.10. Correlations between the entry characteristics and the four intervening variables are appreciably higher.

The background variables do correlate with the intervening variables showing that the way a student attempts to adapt to study is strongly influenced by the pre-entry characteristics, experiences and social patterns of the student. The path model suggests that processes of adaptation and development take place between entry and outcome. The intervening variables in the path model describe and measure these influences on a student's progress during a course of study. The degree of social integration influences the extent or ease of academic integration. This is born out by the manner in which the two social integration variables are related to the academic integration variables. The social integration factor has a significant path to the academic integration factor but not to academic incompatibility. The external attribution factor has a strong correlation to academic incompatibility but only a barely significant one to academic integration. The degree of social integration influences the extent or ease of academic integration. Students who receive support and encouragement from family, friends and employers, which enables them to cope with study in the home, find it easier to come to terms with their academic demands. On the other hand, those students who were unable to reconcile the demands of distance learning courses with their personal lives were more likely to find it difficult to accommodate to academic demands.

The correlation between GPA and persistence criteria is higher in this study of progress in distance education than in comparable studies of courses for on-campus students (e.g., Bean, 1982; Pascarella & Chapman, 1983). The higher correlation is presumably in part due to the differing processes for withdrawal between the modes of study. To cease a full-time course of study requires the completion of a set of procedures and results in an academic record quite distinct from an academic failure. However, distance education students can cease participating in a course, without giving any formal notice of withdrawal, simply by giving up working on their study package or viewing the mediated lessons. The only clue that the institution might have that such informal withdrawals have occurred is that assignments fail to arrive and/or the student does not attend the examination. As no formal withdrawal procedure has been completed, students who cease study in this way will be recorded as having failed the module in which they were enrolled.

This study obtained a much higher figure for the coefficient of determination (R^2) than has been reported for other path studies of drop-out models (e.g., Bernard & Amundsen, 1989; Munro, 1981; Pascarella & Chapman, 1983; Sweet, 1986).The obtained value implies that 80% of the total variance of student persistence could be explained by the variables in the model. However, a large portion of the variance arises from the inclusion of GPA in the path model. The coefficient of determination for GPA is considerably less. The other four intervening variables have low coefficients, which suggests that there are other factors not considered in the model having a more substantial influence on these variables (indicated by the error terms).

Conclusion

Overall the path model shows a good fit to the model derived from the qualitative data. To add further confirmation to the model, the next step was to perform a replication test on a discrete sample of students. This is the subject of the next chapter.

Chapter 12

Replication Test

Synopsis

Following the initial test of the DESP instrument, items which did not contribute to scales were deleted. Extra items were added to some sub-scales in a bid to increase reliability. The revised version of the instrument was then used with students enrolled in three different programs. Reliabilities of scales and sub-scales were compared to those in the original study. The path model relating scales to entry characteristics and outcome measures was found to be substantially the same as that in the original study, providing strong support for the model.

Replication Test

This chapter reports the results obtained with the DESP inventory from students in three programs, quite discrete from those examined in the original test. Essentially this is a replication study. The aim was to see whether a similar path model for student progress would be found for these three different open learning programs to that found in the original study.

The DESP instrument had produced discrete, easily interpreted factor structures in line with the model. The reliability of the four main scales, as indicated by the Cronbach alpha coefficients, was satisfactory. Most of the sub-scales also had satisfactory alpha coefficients. Some had only two items and alpha values which were moderate to low. The DESP inventory was, therefore, improved by adding extra items to the identified sub-scales. Items which did not load on the factors were dropped. The modifications to the inventory were then to be examined in the replication test by noting the effect on sub-scale and scale reliabilities.

Students and Programs Sampled

This revised version of the DESP questionnaire was administered to students enrolled in open learning programs offered in Hong Kong by three institutions. The programs examined were: a range of courses in arts, science and business offered by the Open Learning Institute of Hong Kong (OLIHK); the B Ed program offered to Hong Kong teachers by Deakin University of Australia; and a post-graduate program offered to student guidance teachers by the Hong Kong Polytechnic. All three programs have been described in Chapter 5. The programs of study are quite discrete from those examined with the original version of the questionnaire. Indeed, two of the three were offered by institutions not concerned with the original study.

The three programs in the study were offered to adult part-time students. They fell within the normally accepted definition of distance education courses (e.g., Keegan, 1986) in that the large majority of the study process takes place in the absence of an on-site teacher. All of the courses supplied students with a study package with a core in the print medium, and some courses used other media including audio and video cassettes and broadcast television. The three programs took advantage of the compact nature of Hong Kong to offer higher levels of face-to-face tutorial support than is usually available for distance education courses.

The sample for the study consisted of all students enrolled in the student guidance and education courses and a 25% random sample of OLIHK students. A sample of OLIHK students was taken because of the relatively large number of students in that program. The total sample consisted of 1087 students. The questionnaires were administered using the same timing and procedures as in the initial test. Usable responses were received from 555 students giving a response rate of 51%.

Variables

As before, the DESP inventory contained measures for background or demographic variables and measures of social and academic integration as reformulated for a distance education context. The number of items for each sub-scale are indicated in Table 12-1, since some items were added to the version of the questionnaire referred to in the previous chapter. Outcome variables, which were GPA and a measure of course completion, were obtained separately from the institutions.

Results

Reliabilities

Table 12-1 examines the reliabilities of sub-scales developed for the DESP inventory. The table gives Cronbach alpha values for reliabilities (SPSS Inc., 1986).

Table 12-1: Number of Items and Reliabilities of Sub-scales in the DESP Inventory

Sub-scale	No. of Items	Reliability
Enrollment encouragement	4	0.46
Study encouragement	4	0.49
Family support	3	0.48
Positive course evaluation	5	0.49
Positive telephone counseling	4	0.76
Reading habit	3	0.53
Insufficient time	4	0.77
Events hinder study	3	0.55
Distractions	7	0.56
Potential drop-out	3	0.66
Negative course evaluation	6	0.66

Comparing reliability values for the original (see Table 11-1) and revised versions of the inventory, it can be seen that seven of the eleven sub-scales have higher reliabilities in the revised version. This indicates an appreciable level of enhancement given that the sub-scales were formed in the original version following the exploratory factor analysis.

Table 12-2 gives reliabilities for the four academic and social integration scales. If Table 11-3 is examined comparison can be made between the original and revised versions. Two scales have higher reliabilities and two lower, with little change in values.

Table 12-2: Reliabilities of Scales in the Replication Study

Scale	Reliability
Social integration	0.67
External attribution	0.68
Academic integration	0.61
Academic incompatibility	0.59

Factor Analysis

Second order factor analysis was conducted using the method of principal component analysis followed by varimax rotation (SPSS Inc., 1986). Items submitted for factor analysis were the eleven sub-scales developed for the DESP inventory, the four sub-scales from the ASI inventory and the English ability sub-scale. These sixteen sub-scales yielded five factors (scales), accounting for 58.5% of the total variance.

Table 12-3 shows the five factor solution. Factor 1 contains the sub-scales of the external attribution factor from the initial study with a small loading from the negative course impression sub-scale. Factor 2 corresponds to the social integration factor in the initial study. The academic integration factor of the original study is split between factors 3 and 5. Factor 3 has the deep approach, intrinsic motivation and reading sub-scales, plus a small negative loading from extrinsic motivation. Factor 5 contains the positive course evaluation and telephone counseling sub-scales. Factor 4 resembles the academic incompatibility factor of the first study, but has no significant loading on extrinsic motivation. Overall, there is little deviation from the factor structure of the original study.

Table 12-3: Second Order Factor Analysis in the Replication Study

Sub-scale / Factor	1	2	3	4	5
Enrollment encouragement		76			
Study encouragement		86			
Family support		37			
Insufficient time	67				
Events hinder study	60				
Distractions	63				
Deep approach			44		
Intrinsic motivation			82		
Reading habit			43		
Positive course evaluation					44
Positive telephone counseling					62
Surface approach				54	
Extrinsic motivation			-34	33	
English ability				47	
Negative course evaluation	39				
Potential drop-out	42				
Eigenvalue	3.33	2.11	1.55	1.30	1.04
% of variance explained	20.8	13.2	9.7	8.2	6.6

Path Analysis

The path model was formed by regressing scales as in the original study. The outcome is shown in Figure 12-1.

Figure 12-1: The Path Model from the Replication Study

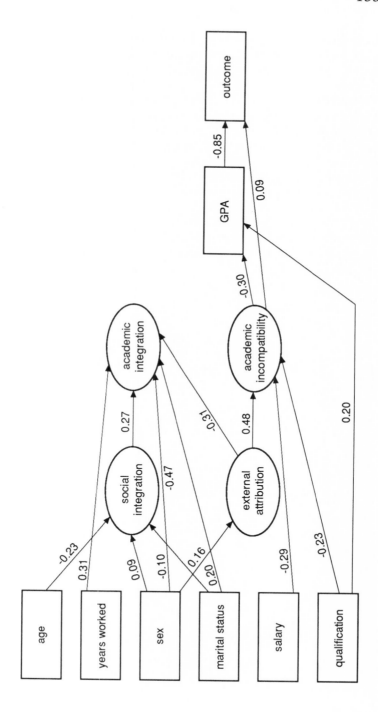

Comparing the significant paths between the four academic and social integration variables and the two outcome variables shows a notable degree of similarity between the two path models.

The original study had paths between academic incompatibility and academic integration, and between external attribution and GPA and outcome which are not in the model for the replication study. The replication study model has a significant path between academic incompatibility and outcome which is not in the original model. However, the path coefficients in each of these three cases are low.

Table 12-4 gives R^2 values and residuals for the intervening and outcome variables in the replication path model. Comparison with values for the original test, given in Table 11-4, shows that the R^2 values for the final outcome variable, the drop-out ratio, are almost equal. With the exception of that for external attribution the remaining R^2 values are higher for the replication study.

Table 12-4: Residuals and R^2 Values for the Replication Path Model

Scale	R^2	Residual
Social integration	0.14	0.93
External attribution	0.03	0.98
Academic integration	0.23	0.88
Academic incompatibility	0.45	0.74
GPA	0.18	0.91
Ratio	0.78	0.47

Conclusion

Like most other models of student persistence this one leaves a large proportion of the variance unexplained. In what is obviously such a complex multi-faceted phenomenon this is hardly surprising.

There is, though, sufficient similarity between the two path models to confirm the substantive findings of the initial study. Two discrete quantitative tests have confirmed a model developed from a wide range of qualitative data. The process of triangulation between quantitative and qualitative data adds markedly to the credibility of the model. The model can, with reasonable confidence, be used to make predictions and derive implications for practice. This is the subject of the remainder of the book.

Part D

Implications for Policy and Practice

Chapter 13

Integration Through Instructional Design

Synopsis

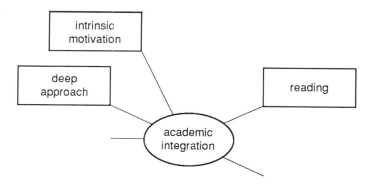

There are policy implications from the model in a number of areas. The positive academic integration factor contains the sub-scales deep approach and intrinsic motivation, while the negative academic incompatibility factor has surface approach and extrinsic motivation. Therefore, if courses wish to enhance student progress, instructional design should concentrate on developing intrinsic motivation and encouraging a deep approach.

The traditional instructional design literature has taken little cognizance of the student learning literature concerning deep and surface approaches. This chapter reviews the two areas of literature and attempts to synthesize some instructional design guidelines for promoting a deep approach and enhancing intrinsic interest. A taxonomy is presented which values student conceptions of key phenomena, and skills for the self-discovery of knowledge, as more important than the accumulation of information. Strategy elements suggested for the selection and sequencing of content focus on revealing the interrelationship between key concepts. Evidence is presented of the persistent nature of existing conceptions and the difficulty of changing conceptual frameworks. Diagnostic questions are suggested as a means of exposing existing conceptions. The next step is to provide a challenge to revealed or anticipated misconceptions so that students pass through a disequilibrium phase before re-forming their existing conceptions.

Preview

The academic integration component of the model has sub-scales for deep approach, intrinsic motivation and positive attitudes towards reading. This chapter considers ways in which the instructional design of courses can enhance these three aspects of academic integration.

Intrinsic motivation and positive attitude to reading are dealt with first. Encouragement of a deep approach through instructional design is then considered at some length, as there is little previous work on this topic.

Motivation

Motivation and interest are very important facets of teaching, but instructional design theorists seem to have had difficulty in prescribing ways to arouse interest and motivation. In an article on the motivational design of instruction, Keller (1983, p. 386) states that:

> .... our understanding of how to arouse and maintain student interest in learning lags far behind our knowledge of how to facilitate learning once the student has the desire to achieve.

Keller, himself, has contributed motivational models for instruction (Keller, 1983; 1987). Keller's original model consisted of four aspects of motivation: interest, relevance, expectancy and satisfaction. For each of the four dimensions of motivation, Keller gives a range of strategies or hints. For example, one of the strategies for interest is (Keller, 1983, p. 403):

> To increase curiosity, use analogies to make the strange *familiar* and the familiar *strange*.

Keller further developed his instructional theories into the "ARCS" model (Keller, 1987). The model specifies four major conditions which need to be met if students are to become and remain motivated: attention, relevance, confidence and satisfaction. Keller suggests strategies for meeting each of these conditions.

I doubt whether motivational models alone are sufficient. In many cases it may be necessary for instructors to undergo a conceptual change in their orientation to teaching, particularly for academics in higher education.

The basis of this assertion is my research with Lyn Gow (Gow & Kember, 1993; Kember & Gow, 1994) on the relationship between orientations to teaching and students' approaches to learning in higher education. Two orientations to teaching were characterized: learning facilitation and knowledge transmission. Mean scores for academic departments for the two orientations were found to correlate with data from longitudinal surveys of students' approaches to learning. Departments with high scores on knowledge transmission discouraged students from adopting a deep approach to study. Departments in which learning facilitation predominated seemed less likely to induce surface approaches.

This research was conducted in a face-to-face teaching situation, but I think it is possible to draw an analogy to open learning courses. Academics holding the knowledge transmission orientation saw knowledge of their subject as a key quality, and conceived their role as imparting that knowledge to students. It is easy to imagine those holding this orientation producing distance education courses which look like academic papers or dry presentations of information.

On the other hand, the learning facilitation orientation had components for interactive teaching, facilitative teaching and motivating students. It is possible to envisage those holding this orientation producing a quite different type of course which takes account of student motivation. Producing interesting courses may, then, require changing the orientations to teaching of instructors. This, though, is not a task to be underestimated, as conceptions can be remarkably tenacious and difficult to change.

Interaction or Transmission

The research discussed above has further implications for the design of instructional systems. Interactive teaching was a key component of the learning facilitation orientation. This suggests that instructional systems and course designs should incorporate interaction between faculty and student, which is not always straightforward in distance education.

The section below suggests ways to incorporate, or at least simulate, interaction into pre-prepared study materials. Better still is a facility for direct communication, which can be either through face-to-face meetings at tutorials or residential schools or through communication channels such as telephone, video links or computer conferencing.

This does not imply, though, that a distance education course with a two-way communication facility is automatically better than one without. As with any use of educational technology, the teaching is more important than the hardware itself. All too often two-way communication channels are not used interactively. They are instead used to deliver a lecture, which means that the teaching orientation is towards information transmission. Williams and Gillard (1986) found that even in tutorials, via a satellite link, the tutors spoke for an average of 81% of the tutorial time and there were frequent periods of lengthy monologue by the tutor.

The conclusion to be drawn is that one-way communication systems are of little value in enhancing motivation. They can do little or nothing which a pre-prepared package cannot. Two-way communication systems provide for interaction which is desirable for both motivation and enhancing a deep approach. However, two-way communication systems only result in interaction if faculty and students use them for discussion purposes. Even the most sophisticated hardware will not guarantee interaction if the faculty insist on lecturing or dominating conversation in a tutorial.

Style of Communication

It is certainly true that instructional designers need to pay greater attention to motivation in developing instructional design models, but greater use could also be made of motivational strategies which have been developed. There are several published sets of guidelines for writers of instructional materials (see, e.g., Fleming & Levie, 1993; Misanchuk, 1992; Rowntree, 1986, ch. 10) suggesting, for example, that study materials use a plain, conversational, informal style of writing. However, many academics continue to use a complex, impersonal style because they feel that such a style is appropriate for academic writing.

An informal conversational style is a facet of the didactic conversational model proposed by Holmberg (1985). Holmberg encourages the use of invitations to exchange views and debate issues, and advocates a writing style employing personal pronouns and colloquial language. The aim is to produce a course which simulates interaction between the course writer and the student. I find a helpful analogy is that of a tutor sitting over the shoulder of the student guiding and discussing the course.

A number of authors have described orientations in study guides, for their particular disciplines, which ought to enhance collective affiliation. Finkel (1985) believes that History courses should be lively and provocative. Nation (1987) talks of "engaging" students in a Sociology course. Shott (1985) advocates the use of audio tapes "in the style of an informal, one-to-one chat to the student" for Physics courses. These approaches can be subsumed within Holmberg's (1985) concept of guided didactic conversation.

Using such an approach can develop a sense of collective affiliation between the student and the instructor, even if the instructor appears in print. Use of non-print media can make it easier to develop a relationship between instructor and students. The same principles do need to be applied, though. A lucid, informal style of writing should help in the development of positive attitudes towards reading. It is not realistic to expect all academics to develop a Shakespearean quality in their prose, but they can at least strive for clarity and brevity.

Authors and instructional designers of higher education open learning courses might profitably learn from the techniques employed by the writers and producers of children's books. Many children demand to be read their favorite books over and over again. How many of our distance education students return to their study guides with such alacrity?

There is wide agreement that diagrams and pictures can be effective both as learning aids and motivational elements and there are a number of guidelines for their use in instructional material (see, e.g., Brody, 1982). Of the many distance education courses which appear without diagrams or pictures some, at least, would benefit from their inclusion.

> In general, the notes are presented well. The varied letter sizes, and the pictures interest me when reading the materials. (Hong Kong–Student Guidance)

Use of a variety of media has also been suggested as a way of enhancing interest and motivation. Rowntree (1986, p. 233) believes that:

> It is both possible and desirable that they should use other media as well. For one thing, the additional media may enable certain kinds of understanding that would not otherwise be possible. Furthermore, the variety–the change of stimulus itself–may refresh and invigorate the learner.

Yet a large proportion of distance education courses still use print alone. There are also telecourses which restrict instruction to the television delivery medium.

Flexibility of Courses and Interest to Students

Fransson (1977) found that students are likely to use a surface approach when they have little interest in the subject matter or do not perceive its relevance to their needs. The provision of freedom of learning and courses relevant to student needs implies flexibility and a range of options within courses. Recognizing that adult students should play a part in selecting the content of their course is also one of the fundamental principles of andragogy (Knowles, 1970; 1984). Adult students are seen as having the maturity to recognize their own learning needs.

Distance education courses, though, frequently offer less flexibility and fewer options than face-to-face teaching. It is easy to negotiate individual study paths with on-campus students as long as there is a reasonable staff/student ratio. However, the provision of flexibility within distance education courses requires extra investment in producing a package of study materials with optional streams and higher levels of academic support to mark the diverse assignments and tutor the options. Providing a wider range of modules within a distance education course also requires considerable investment; the initial expenditure in producing good quality distance education course materials is high.

A Deep Approach Through Instructional Design

The remainder of this chapter proposes guidelines for encouraging a deep approach to learning through the instructional design of courses. Existing research and instructional design theories are examined to see if there are any coherent instructional guidelines which might assist in producing more meaningful learning or encouraging students to employ a deep approach.

Students adapt their approaches to learning according to the content and the context of the learning task. There are a number of results in the literature which show how students can be influenced towards a surface approach. Observations of students making heavy use of reproductive approaches have been found to coincide with factors such as: high workloads (Dahlgren, 1978; 1984); surface level assessment demands (Entwistle & Ramsden, 1983, ch. 8; Thomas & Bain, 1984); low levels of intrinsic interest in the course (Fransson, 1977); and lack of freedom in the learning environment (Ramsden & Entwistle, 1981).

A reduction in the number of students employing a surface approach has intrinsic merit. It not only offers the prospect of increasing pass rates but is also consistent with the traditional goals of tertiary education. Graduates from universities, and even high schools, surely ought to have abandoned habitual rote learning in favor of more meaning-oriented learning approaches. Programs attempting to reorient students away from a surface approach are therefore doubly attractive.

The traditional instructional design literature has not, to any great extent, drawn upon the student learning research which has given rise to the wide interest in deep and surface approaches to learning. It is, therefore, difficult for instructors to find guidelines for encouraging a deep approach to learning in the traditional instructional design literature.

In an analysis of the current status of instructional design, Reigeluth (1989, p. 74), the editor of *Instructional-design theories and models* (1983), asserts that instructional theorists have largely ignored learning characterized by understanding and developed relatively little in the way of validated prescriptions for facilitating understanding. Such a statement would suggest that instructional design theories contain little which would help a teacher who wanted to design instruction which facilitated deep rather than surface learning. By making this assertion Reigeluth was undoubtedly undervaluing both his own work and that of others such as Ausubel, which is referred to in this chapter.

Generalizations are often difficult but in this instance can be further confounded by alternative stances on what are, or are not, instructional design theories. Similarly with the assertion in a recent review of instructional design theories (Merrill, Li & Jones, 1990) that current instructional design theories are firmly rooted in behavioral psychology. However, it is clear that comprehensive instructional design prescriptions have been easier to derive from earlier behavioral theories than from constructivist theories of cognitive psychology (e.g., Schuell, 1986) or research into student learning, which has recognized the desirability of promoting meaningful learning.

The Importance of Conceptions and Skills

To design instruction to facilitate meaningful learning it is first necessary to deal with the issue of what is to be covered by the course of instruction. For this purpose it is useful to have some rationale for deciding between alternative objectives or areas of content, and making decisions about what should be included and what left out. Such decisions can be made as value judgments based upon a simple taxonomy of objectives.

Suitable taxonomies have been proposed, apparently independently, though they are very similar, by Marton (1989) and Sparkes (1989). Marton (1989) identified three kinds of competence which educational institutions might aim to develop; conceptions, skills and knowledge. Marton defines conceptions as how students *perceive* and *understand* important phenomena in their discipline. Skills are what the students can *do*, in other words the procedures they can carry out. The final category is what the students *know*, so it is the factual knowledge they possess. This taxonomy is neither as detailed as others nor as precise, since individuals can place different interpretations upon the phrase "important phenomena" used in the definition of conceptions.

Sparkes (1989) also divides objectives into three categories and uses identical labels to Marton for two of the three. *Knowledge,* is defined as information committed to memory, and *skills* as the ability to do specific things without necessarily understanding the underlying processes. Sparkes' (p. 3) third category is "the deeper learning variously described as *understanding,* or *conceptual learning,* or *meaningful learning.*" Understanding is Sparkes' preferred term, which he describes as "grasping concepts and being able to use them creatively" (p. 4).

The classifications of these taxonomies can serve as a guide for judgments about what a curriculum should concentrate upon. Marton argues that educational institutions should place priority on developing student conceptions, as these provide a framework for the development of skills and knowledge. If a course is to be oriented towards meaningful learning, then it ought to focus on the key concepts of the subject area. In planning a course, an instructional designer or instructor might ask "what are the most important concepts?" The course would then be sequenced to focus first on the most important concepts, and concentrate on ensuring that students have an appropriate understanding or conception of key issues. There may not be complete agreement among experts as to what are the key concepts in a discipline, so different courses may well concentrate on somewhat different concepts. In most disciplines, though, there should be a distinction between key concepts and factual information.

A case can also be made for valuing skills more highly than knowledge. Factual information is an increasingly transient commodity. In many disciplines the information base has grown dramatically, but the relevance half-life is falling continuously. Students, therefore, need to be equipped with the fundamental skills of their discipline so that they can discover for themselves the information they need.

Developing a thorough understanding takes time, even if the course is largely constrained to key concepts. As the time available for courses is finite, time spent altering conceptions is likely to be at the expense of covering details. Roth and Anderson (1988) compare case-studies of two teachers covering the same part of a course on light and seeing, using the same textbook. The first teacher went through the whole section of the textbook and covered every concept. However, at the end of the course only 15% of the students had developed an understanding of how light enables you to see, and could apply their understanding to everyday phenomena. By contrast the teacher in the second case-study aimed for conceptual change so concentrated on key concepts at the expense of covering the entire section of the textbook. In the post-test 64% of her class had developed an understanding of seeing.

A decrease in content of many courses should be of little concern since information is becoming outdated at an ever increasing pace. Rather than attempting to build a knowledge base, courses might concentrate on teaching students to become self-managed learners so that they can keep themselves abreast of subsequent developments.

Workload

Concentrating upon important concepts rather than covering content is doubly important as there is evidence that heavy workload tends to promote the use of a surface approach. In a study of first-year economics students (Dahlgren, 1978; Dahlgren & Marton, 1978), it was found that few students had truly grasped the technical meaning of basic concepts by the end of the course. Dahlgren (1978) related the lack of understanding to the overwhelming nature of the curriculum. Faced with the large quantity of knowledge, students tended to abandon the search for meaning and resorted to memorizing algorithmic procedures for answering problems in order to pass examinations.

Ramsden and Entwistle (1981) related the results from a large survey of students using the Approaches to Studying inventory to the students' perceptions of the teaching in their departments. It was found that departments which scored highly on good teaching, allowed freedom in student learning, and did not impose excessive workloads had a higher than average proportion of students who displayed a meaning orientation.

Excessive workloads may have a magnified impact on part-time adult students who are able to devote only a limited proportion of their time to study. Adult educators should therefore be particularly zealous in seeking out courses with an unreasonable workload. The research evidence suggests that reducing the content of overloaded courses should result in an increase in the quality of learning even if the quantity of factual material covered is reduced.

Sequence

When an instructor has identified important conceptions it is then necessary to decide a sequence for teaching them. The best developed and most relevant theory for this purpose is elaboration theory (Reigeluth, 1979; Reigeluth & Stein, 1983; Reigeluth, Merrill, Wilson & Spiller, 1980). Reigeluth introduces elaboration theory with an analogy to a zoom lens. Elaboration theory suggests that a subject is first viewed through a wide-angle lens to get a view of the major aspects of the picture and the relationship between them. The lens can then zoom in on a part of the scene to examine the detail. The analogy is not a perfect one, as Reigeluth recognizes (1979, p. 9), because wider angle lenses have greater depth of focus so more detail is visible. The analogy would be better if wide angle lenses had narrow depths of field so only the main items were in focus, and the small details were blurred.

Reigeluth (1979) prescribes either general to detailed or simple to complex sequences for elaboration theory. These sequencing continua also seem appropriate if instructional designs are to concentrate on meaningful learning. A course should start with the fundamental concepts and fill in the details later. Otherwise students may fail to identify the key concepts and distinguish them from the supporting detail.

If a deep approach is to be promoted, it is suggested that the amount of detail to be included be kept to a minimum, especially in view of the above evidence that heavy workloads tend to be linked to a surface approach. The emphasis should be on the *quality* of learning rather than *quantity*. An instructional designer should constantly ask, "what can be left out?" Instead of providing complete coverage of a subject it would be more fruitful to teach students the skills necessary for applying the information to solve novel problems and discovering information for themselves. For this reason the skills category, of Marton's (1989) or Sparkes' (1989) taxonomy, is seen as superior to the knowledge classification, especially skills related to discovering relevant information.

A recent review of elaboration theory (Wilson & Cole, 1992) suggests revisions to the theory which make it more usable for instruction aimed at understanding. Wilson and Cole believe that the theory should be treated more as a set of principles than as a procedural approach, as the detailed prescriptions of the original model impose unnecessary design constraints. They also suggest that organization and sequencing be based on learners' understanding as well as the logical structure of the subject matter. This latter recommendation is more consistent with the position taken here on the importance of the learner's conceptions of key concepts. In a comment on Wilson and Cole's recommendations, Reigeluth (1992) was generally supportive and suggested that some of the recommendations had already been incorporated into revisions of the original theory.

Reigeluth, Merrill, Wilson and Spiller (1980) suggest that the zoom lens approach, or top-down sequencing strategies, has not been widely employed. They suggest that instruction more commonly commences with a detailed examination of minor topics, possibly influenced by Gagné's (1968) hierarchical sequencing theory. Bottom-up approaches are also more common at the curriculum design level. Many courses follow the "bricks building a wall" approach. The initial part of the course is devoted to building up a factual knowledge base, often of supporting subjects. It is only in the final stages of courses, of this nature, that students face challenges which examine their understanding and ability to apply concepts fundamental to their chosen discipline. It is often difficult for students taking such courses to see how the initial bricks will fit together to build the wall. They can lose interest in the course because they seem to be studying subjects which do not relate to their chosen course. The problem is magnified for part-time students, like the one making the comment below, as the precursor subjects extend over a greater period.

> So far we have only covered the fundamental courses. I still couldn't see the whole picture yet. However, I haven't seen any electronics courses offered yet as was announced by the institute earlier. (Hong Kong–OLIHK)

Another problem with beginning instruction with the minor precursor topics is that students often fail to distinguish the main concepts or principles from the supporting material. The term *horizontalization* can be used to describe the process by which students fail to distinguish fundamental concepts from subsidiary material. The term has previously been used (Marton & Wenestam, 1978; Wenestam, 1978) when students reading a text confuse or do not distinguish the principle from the example.

Courses which start by building a knowledge base can also obscure the fundamental nature of a discipline, or fail to teach students the skills of practitioners in the subject area. Unless early conceptions of the nature of their discipline are explicitly challenged, students can cling to inappropriate views and corresponding approaches. For example students might still believe that in history one remembers dates (Hallden, 1986) or in geography place names, while their teachers are concerned with objectives classified as analysis, synthesis or evaluation.

Links Between Concepts

For learning to be meaningful, students must not only have a genuine understanding of the most important concepts, but should also be able to relate one concept to another. However, a number of studies (e.g., Champagne *et al.*, 1981; 1985; Novak & Gowin, 1984; West, Fensham & Garrard, 1985) have shown that students are often unaware of the relationship between concepts or fail to relate them to their existing knowledge base.

The strategy element which has most commonly been used to reveal links between concepts is the advance organizer, developed primarily by Ausubel (1960; 1968). Melton (1984, p. 61) believes that an advance organizer can be described in terms of two principal characteristics.

> First, it should provide a clear and well-organized framework, or 'ideational scaffolding,' for the assimilation of the subsequent learning. Secondly, this ideational scaffolding should become attached to, and integrated within, the learner's existing cognitive structure, thus contributing to the development and clarification of the structure and hence to learning.

There have been many studies of the effects of advance organizers upon learning. Barnes and Clawson (1975) did a meta-analysis of 32 studies of advance organizers. Their analysis used a simple voting procedure. Since 20 of the studies failed to produce significant results, Barnes and Clawson concluded that advance organizers did not facilitate learning. A more thorough meta-analysis by Luiten, Ames and Ackerson (1980) located 134 studies of the effect of advance organizers on student learning. They used more sophisticated meta-analytic techniques, which yielded an average effect size of 0.21, resulting in a quite different conclusion to Barnes and Clawson (1975).

The analysis by Barnes and Clawson, and more particularly the research on which it drew, has been criticized on several grounds. Lawton and Wanska (1977) pointed out that advance organizers would not help learning if the students did not make use of the advance organizer, or already possessed the relevant ideational scaffolding. Ausubel (1978) criticized many studies for failing to distinguish meaningful from non-meaningful learning. He observed that many of the studies had used verbatim recall of knowledge as the measurement criteria, yet advance organizers are designed to facilitate meaningful learning. Similarly Mayer (1979) asserted that many of the experiments had measured "amount retained." His assimilation theory predicted that advance organizers would enhance the learning of conceptual ideas but not of technical details.

Meta-analysis of research into advance organizers therefore suggests that they have a small positive effect. Criticism of the research on which the meta-analysis is based suggests that greater benefits are likely to occur if advance organizers are used for conceptual or meaningful learning. The use of advance organizers, therefore, seems to be justified if instruction is designed to facilitate conceptual change learning or promote a deep approach.

Graphic Organizers

Advance organizers are normally in written form and have a wider role than purely showing the relationship between key concepts. Graphic organizers or structured overviews are more specifically related to showing conceptual relationships. In essence they are graphic representations of the relationships between the principal concepts in a subject area.

The strategy element is not yet operationally defined in a form which has been consistently accepted. Barron (1969) used the term *structured overview* to refer to tree diagrams linking main concepts in a hierarchical relationship. Hawk, McLeod and Jonassen (1985) and Morris and Stewart-Dore (1984) reserve the term structured overview for these tree diagrams linking key concepts. They use the terms *graphic organizer* or *graphic outline* for more diverse pictorial representations of the relationships between concepts, most of which require students to place information into spaces left in the diagrams. These graphic outlines seem promising for promoting meaningful learning since they involve students in actively constructing their own representations of content structures. The learning process also becomes generative rather than declarative (Jonassen, 1985) so promotes an ability to seek and distinguish relationships between concepts.

In a meta-analysis Moore and Readence (1984) seem to use the term graphic organizer to subsume any graphic portrayal of the relationship between concepts, yet most of the studies they examined used tree diagrams. The meta-analysis concluded that use of structured overviews increased student performance by an average effect size of 0.22 standard deviations. For experiments involving university students the mean effect size was 0.66, possibly because they were more able to make effective use of the structured overviews.

There seems to be reasonable evidence that advance organizers, and the sub-set structured overviews, do facilitate learning. Their effect seems most pronounced when meaningful learning is desired, so their inclusion, is particularly recommended in the present context.

Using both prose advance organizers and structured overviews for the same lesson segments seems justifiable. Some students prefer textual presentation of information, others graphic or iconic. Still others will find that a combination of textual and graphic presentations will provide optimum clarity in revealing conceptual links. Research is needed on the use of combinations of prose advance organizers and structured overviews for revealing conceptual links and promoting meaningful learning. The most likely outcome is that students will use only those strategy elements which appear to them to be useful, simply skipping over either or both advance organizer or structured overview if it does not seem to aid their learning. In a diary study of the way distance learning students worked through a self-study module, Clyde *et al.* (1983) found a wide variety of study sequences and pathways. Few students stuck to the study sequence suggested by the instructor.

Diagnosing Conceptions

Research into student misconceptions shows that merely presenting a concept is insufficient if genuine understanding is desired. Students can be taught the relevant concepts, possibly

several times, yet their conceptions can be diametrically opposed
to the concepts they were taught (Osborne & Wittrock, 1983).
Clearly it is difficult to introduce new conceptions, alter existing
conceptions or replace naive conceptions with more sophisticated
ones.

In some instances the teaching may have inadequately
distinguished the key concepts from the supporting detail. There
may also have been insufficient attention to revealing the links
between the key concepts. Concentrating on concepts, if
necessary at the expense of detail, and adopting simple to
complex sequences will help the students identify the concepts.
Advance organizers and structured overviews have already been
suggested as strategy elements for revealing links between
concepts. However, neither these strategy elements nor the
sequencing guidelines are likely to be sufficient to cause students
to change deeply held conceptions.

Champagne, Gunstone and Klopher (1985) do report changes in
student conceptions of physics phenomena after several day-long
sessions of ideational conflict, but quotations from some of the
students illustrate the demanding nature of the process. In a
wider context, the pioneering work of Lewin (1952) on bringing
about social change through group decision making suggests a
three-step procedure: unfreezing, moving and freezing of a level.
Nussbaum and Novick (1982) and West (1988) suggest that, in
an educational context, a similar three phase process is required
to bring about conceptual change.

1.   A process for diagnosing existing conceptual frameworks
     and revealing them to the student.

2.   A period of disequilibrium and conceptual conflict which
     makes students dissatisfied with existing conceptions.

3.   A reconstruction or reforming phase in which a new
     conceptual framework is formed.

The first step towards conceptual change is, therefore, the
identification of existing conceptions. The strategy elements
selected are questions of the type used in research into student
conceptions and misconceptions of fundamental concepts. The
questions should pose a genuine test of the students' understanding
of the concept. It should not be possible to answer the questions by

re-stating a remembered definition of the concept or by using a standard algorithmic procedure to substitute values into formulae.

Questions

As the diagnostic questions demand meaningful responses rather than the recall of information, they should contribute towards the encouragement of a deep approach or, at least, the discouragement of a surface approach, in addition to identifying student conceptions. There is clear evidence (Entwistle & Ramsden, 1983; Marton & Säljö, 1976b; Thomas & Bain, 1984; Watkins & Hattie, 1981) that setting assessment items which demand surface level responses inevitably leads to the wider adoption of surface approaches.

Marton and Säljö (1976b) asked two groups of students to read a series of three articles. After each reading one group was asked questions on the underlying meaning of the article, the other group was asked about factual detail. Students in the latter group, who habitually employed a deep approach, tended to adopt a surface approach in the face of persistent factual questions. However, surface learners who were asked meaning oriented questions did not adopt a true deep approach but tried to remember summaries of the author's arguments without actively examining them. The conclusion derived from the experiment was that a surface approach was easy to induce with factual questions whereas persuading surface learners to adopt a deep approach was not an easy task. Kember and Gow (1989) speculated that it may be those students with an inadequate conception of learning who fail to utilize deep strategies in response to higher order questions.

Open learning study materials often use in-text or adjunct questions as mathemagenic activators (Rothkopf, 1965, p. 198). There are a number of guidelines for their use based on research into the effect of inserted questions on learning from reading tasks (e.g., Kember, 1985). The work of Marton and Säljö (1976b) should also be taken into account when using in-text questions. If the questions consistently ask for nothing more than the recall of factual information, then students might reasonably assume that the course demands memorization of details and resort to rote learning. If higher order skills such as application, analysis, synthesis or evaluation are really desired, then the questions in the study guide should demand responses which require students to use those same skills.

Sources of Questions and Alternative Conceptions

How are teachers to deduce questions which will reveal
conceptions of important phenomena and how will they deduce
likely alternative conceptions? Phenomenographic research into
student learning (e.g., Marton, Hounsell & Entwistle, 1984) and
research into students misconceptions of science concepts (e.g.,
West & Pines, 1985) suggests that it will be possible to classify
the responses to such questions into a small number (usually
between two and five) of categories which correspond to
alternative conceptions.

There is now a reasonably extensive and growing body of
research into student conceptions of phenomena. These often
provide examples of questions used in the research and show
revealed misconceptions. A thorough review of this body of
research would be too extensive for this chapter. General
examinations of the literature are provided by West and Pines
(1985) and by Ramsden (1988). Sources for science, in general,
are Driver and Erickson (1983), Helm and Novak (1983), Pfundt
and Druit (1985) and West and Pines (1985). The bulk of the
research is in science with physics receiving particular attention
(e.g., McDermott, 1984). Interpretation of basic algebra was
investigated by Lochhead (1985). In chemistry, student
understanding of the mole concept (e.g. Lybeck *et al.*, 1988) and
topics such as phase diagrams (e.g., West, Fensham & Garrard,
1985) have been examined.

There have been fewer investigations in the arts and social
sciences. Halldén (1986) and Hounsell (1984) examined student
conceptions of the nature of the history discipline. Dahlgren
(1978; 1984) examined conceptions of price held by economics
students. Medical teaching has also been fruitful for research into
student learning (e.g., Eizenberg, 1986; Newble & Clarke, 1987).

Although the research into students' alternative conceptions of
phenomena is quite extensive, it certainly does not cover every
key concept in every discipline, and almost certainly never will.
Ramsden (1987) has suggested that instructors should be helped
to do research into their own students' learning to discover
misconceptions for themselves. While this aim is to be
encouraged, not all teachers will possess the desire, expertise and
time to conduct such research. Those who do are unlikely to have
the time to thoroughly research every concept in every course they
teach.

It is not necessary for all the questions and alternative conceptions to be derived from research. Bowden (1988) describes a workshop for instructors in which participants are asked to create a question to elicit student understanding of key phenomenon in their discipline. Further the teachers are expected to suggest likely answers to the question which will reveal alternative conceptions held by students. An example is given (Bowden, 1988, p. 262) of how some participants responded to this activity.

> Electricity: You are an electron in the middle of a copper wire. At a certain time, I will connect a battery across your wire. How will you react before and after connection?

> My neighbor bumps me immediately and then I bump the neighbor on the other side.

> I sit still before connection but gradually move together with the others after connection.

> I gradually accelerate.

> I take off with the speed of light.

> Before connection, I am dancing around randomly. I do not feel the field from the battery immediately, but when it gets here (at the speed of light) my dance is biased a bit in the direction of the field.

Bowden (1989) asserts that, after participation in the workshop, good teachers are able to draw upon their teaching experiences to deduce questions which portray student conceptions and misconceptions of fundamental concepts. They are also likely to be able to predict how the more common misconceptions will be revealed in answers to these questions. It is a common practice for teachers to note mistaken ideas which arise in classroom discussion, or common mistakes in assignments. Parts of tutorials are often devoted to attempting to rectify the most frequent errors in the last assignment. The practice of looking for and trying to remedy common mistakes is therefore nothing novel to many teachers.

Challenging and Reforming Conceptions

Assuming an appropriate question has been selected, and incorrect or inadequate conceptions have been revealed, it is then necessary to provide a challenge and feedback to students who have revealed inappropriate conceptions. As the incorrect responses are likely to correspond to intuitive or deep-seated convictions, merely indicating that the response is incorrect, and giving the correct answer, is unlikely to alter the student's conception. There is no doubt that the process of conceptual change is difficult (e.g., Champagne, Gunstone & Klopfer, 1985). Strike and Posner (1985) characterize cognitive change in terms of advances, retreats and periods of indecision. As suggested above, the students need to go through phases of disequilibrium and then reconceptualization.

The feedback to inappropriate responses should aim to expose the incongruity of the existing beliefs. Students should be asked to consider the inconsistencies between the position resulting from their exposed or diagnosed beliefs and that from established wisdom. Real world examples and counter-examples, following from the scenarios established in the initial question, are more likely to be effective than abstract theoretical feedback.

The process of challenging conceptions needs to be thorough, and is, therefore, a time-consuming process. Firstly there may be several alternative conceptions to challenge. The cited electricity example, taken from Bowden (1988), has four alternative conceptions to be dealt with. Each alternative conception should be challenged, either individually or jointly, if that is possible. In the electricity example some of the alternative responses are related.

Conceptual change teaching has been operationalized in a number of diverse ways. The most common approach has involved extensive discussion sessions. Champagne, Gunstone and Klopfer (1985) report a workshop in which each student is asked to explain a common physical situation. Individual students then present their analyses to the class. Discussion or debate follows as the analyses differ and controversies arise. Watts and Bentley (1987) discuss the teacher characteristics conducive to creating a non-threatening learning environment which they consider important for facilitating conceptual change.

It is at this stage of the instructional process that live interaction is most advantageous. If the course is media based, any available tutorial time would be most advantageously devoted to discussion sessions aimed towards ideational confrontation. If tutorial time were not available, the discussion would have to be simulated in print or through computer software.

Various aids to the change process have been employed. Gunstone and White (1981) made use of demonstrations to promote conceptual change in physics students. Roth and Anderson (1988) describe ways in which teachers can use science textbooks to enhance meaningful learning in the classroom. White and Horwitz (1988) explain how students can test their conceptions of mechanics with computer simulations.

Example

To illustrate the teaching of fundamental conceptions two contrasting activities, taken from Kember and Murphy (1994), will be discussed.

An elephant weighing 40 000 N has feet of area 1000 cm^2 (= 0.1 m). What is the pressure on the ground?

pressure $\quad = \dfrac{\text{force}}{\text{area}}$

$\quad\quad\quad\quad\quad = \dfrac{40\ 000\ \text{N}}{4 \times 0.1\ \text{m}^2}$

$\quad\quad\quad\quad\quad = 100\ 000\ \text{Nm}^{-2}$

$\quad\quad\quad\quad\quad = 1 \times 10^5\ \text{Pa}$

(Kember and Murphy, 1993, p. 73)

Questions like this are very common. Students normally answer them by an algorithmic approach. They decide which of the formulae they have remembered is appropriate. They work out which numbers correspond to the variables in the formula and substitute into the equation. From then on it is simply an algebraic exercise.

There is nothing fundamentally wrong with problems of this type. They do provide practice in manipulating data and solving numerical problems. The one above requires an understanding of powers of ten and the use of units. However, it should not be assumed that successfully solving a numerical exercise implies an understanding of the concepts represented by the equation. A student could solve the above problem without having any real understanding of pressure, force or mass.

Now consider an alternative activity which might stimulate thought about the underlying concepts. A single activity may not be enough to change a strongly held conception but if a course concentrates on fundamental concepts and activities of this latter type predominate then conceptual change is possible.

> If a lady wearing stiletto heeled shoes and an elephant walk across a piece of soft ground, which is likely to leave the deepest footprints?

> Your immediate reaction may well have been the elephant. The elephant would have a greater mass than the lady. The total force or weight that it exerts on the ground would be greater than the lady's. But is it really appropriate to consider just the weight?

> You may have started to think about how the forces are applied. Elephants have big feet. Their large weight would therefore be distributed over a reasonably big area. The lady's weight, though, would all be applied through the very small area of the stiletto heel.

> Which is the appropriate physical concept to apply?

> Try using the following data to determine which does the most damage. An elephant weighing 40 000 N has feet of area 1000 cm^2 (= 0.1m). A lady weighing 400 N has stiletto heels of area 1 cm^2 (1 x 10^{-4} m^2).

> To determine the depth to which the foot and heel will sink you need to consider the area over which the force is applied. The elephant is very heavy but the force is applied through its large feet. The effect on the ground is spread out over a large area. The weight of the lady, however, is concentrated onto the point of the stiletto heels. Her weight is less but it acts through a much smaller area.

Pressure is the physical quantity which relates force and area of contact. If you have not already done so, work out the pressure applied by the elephant and the lady.

elephant   **lady**

pressure $= \dfrac{\text{force}}{\text{area}}$ pressure $= \dfrac{\text{force}}{\text{area}}$

$= \dfrac{40\ 000\ \text{N}}{4 \times 0.1\ \text{m}^2}$ $= \dfrac{400\ \text{N}}{2 \times 1 \times 10^{-4}\ \text{m}^2}$

$= 100\ 000\ \text{Nm}^{-2}$ $= 200 \times 10^4\ \text{Nm}^{-2}$

$= 1 \times 10^5\ \text{Pa}$ $= 2 \times 10^6\ \text{Pa}$

The elephant exerts larger *force* because it is much heavier, but the lady's heel exerts a much bigger *pressure* because of its smaller area! The lady's heel would sink further into the ground.

(Kember and Murphy, 1994, p. 74-76)

If conceptual change is to occur, students' existing conceptions need to be challenged by a variety of problems related to the concept. By working through a series of questions, there will be an opportunity for existing conceptions to be destabilized and replaced by more sophisticated conceptions. If deep-seated convictions are to be challenged, it will be necessary to pose several questions for each important concept. Driver and Oldham (1985) see a constructivist teaching sequence as needing a loop. Students need to repeat the sequence of evaluating then clarifying their beliefs against alternative conceptual frameworks. By posing a series of questions, students challenge and reform their conceptions. In Strike and Posner's (1985) terms, there are chances to advance and retreat.

From a more general perspective, efforts to challenge and reform student conceptions can be seen as part of the process of aiding student intellectual development through the nine positions identified by Perry (1970; 1988). Perry characterized students' cognitive and intellectual development by observed positions ranging from the unswerving belief in the correctness of authorities, through a more relativistic understanding, to the ability to evolve and evaluate personal commitments. Perry (1988) sees a role for the teacher in assisting students to develop through the positions by combinations of challenge and support,

which clearly resembles the processes for conceptual change
discussed earlier.

Conclusion

It should by now be obvious that I have a strong orientation
towards devising courses which encourage students to adopt a
deep approach. The model provides support for this position
because deep approach and intrinsic motivation are important
facets of the academic integration component on the positive
track of the model. Encouraging a deep approach and intrinsic
motivation are also consistent with the aims of most higher
education courses, and indeed the majority of courses at any
educational level.

However, traditional instructional design theory has little to say
about how to encourage a deep approach. Indeed, some of the
behaviorally based theories may do much to promote surface
learning, even if not intended by the designers. There is, then, a
need to broaden the influences upon instructional design theories
to include work from constructivism and research into student
learning. This chapter has provided one attempt to synthesize
some of these other influences with more appropriate work on
instructional design.

In general the strategies selected have been those suitable for pre-
prepared instructional packages as there is already an extensive
literature on promoting a deep approach in conventional face-to-
face teaching. The desirability is recognized of having a channel
for two-way communication between faculty and students in
open learning courses. If this communication channel is to
contribute to promoting a deep approach it should be used for
interaction and discussion and not for the transmission of
information.

Fortunately there does now seem to be a recognition that
instructional design theories do need to draw upon wider
influences and work derived from constructivism (e.g., Garrison,
1993; Schoenfield, 1992), cognitive science (e.g., Biggs, 1991;
Bonner, 1988), and student learning research (e.g., Kember, 1991)
has begun to appear. Seels (in press) is also editing a book which
reconsiders fundamental impacts on instructional design by
taking into account these wider perspectives.

Chapter 14

Academic Integration Through Tutorial Support

Synopsis

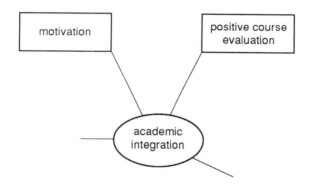

The model suggests that persistence and performance in open learning situations can be improved if academic integration is enhanced. For tutoring and student support services this can be accomplished through either developing collective affiliation or by ensuring normative congruence between student expectations and course procedures.

Collective affiliation can be developed through any of the communication channels between the institution and the student. Sessions between a tutor and a group of students seem to be particularly valued. Other communications, including those of an administrative nature, all play a part in forming the students' vision of the institution.

Normative congruence can be difficult for adult students with limited previous study experience. There is often a mis-match between the students' conception of study requirements and the conventions and

norms of academia. Entry programs which help students adjust to
academic expectations can be of value. The format of such entry
programs is discussed.

Academic Environment and Integration

For the purposes of the model the academic environment is
defined as embracing all facets of the offering of an open learning
course by an institution. It, therefore, includes both academic and
administrative support systems, the package of study materials
and any lessons delivered via television, computer networks or by
other audio-visual or multimedia formats. This is clearly the
component of the model over which the institution would have
the greatest control so there should be an opportunity of
enhancing the academic integration of students.

The integration aspects of the model are based on Durkheim's
(1961) model of suicide, which suggested that suicide was more
likely to happen if integration had not occurred. The two forms of
integration cited were collective affiliation and value integration,
or normative congruence. Academic integration will be considered
according to these two sub-divisions.

The previous chapter dealt with enhancing academic integration
through the instructional system, that is, with a study package or
content delivered through telecommunication channels. This
chapter is concerned with academic support networks. By this I
mean tutorials, telephone tutorials or residential schools held
with the aim of assisting the student to understand the content
delivered in the study package or telecommunicated lessons.

Collective Affiliation

Collective affiliation means, in this context, that students feel
that they are an integral part of the college. It is their college and
they are a valued member of it. Mahony and Morgan (1991) refer
to a "sense of belonging," which they interpret as an umbrella
term encompassing issues of affiliation, status and recognition.
They suggest that these factors do have an influence on drop-out
rates.

The obvious corollary is that colleges should try to make their
students feel that they belong and that they are valued members

of college society. Unfortunately, achieving collective affiliation can be difficult in distance education when the college is far from the student.

> There is no sense of belonging because geographically Deakin is very far from us. (Hong Kong–Education)

> No, because I don't even have any idea of what the university looks like. I might pay a visit there one day. (Hong Kong–Education)

Many students enroll in open learning courses based in their own city because they cannot attend regular classes. Even when their college is quite close, though, it is difficult to generate the same sense of belonging that a full-time on-campus student might feel.

> Being a distance learner in the Hong Kong Polytechnic, my feeling of a sense of belonging is very little because I only come for the tutorial once a month. In addition to that I seldom use the Polytechnic facilities. (Hong Kong–Textiles)

> Even though I am a distance learning student here, I don't feel any sense of belonging because the Polytechnic cannot provide many facilities for us; unlike part-time evening students where regular classes meet every week. (Hong Kong–Textiles)

In generating a sense of belonging, distance learning institutions clearly start with a handicap as compared to campus colleges. If collective affiliation is to be achieved, the distance learning institution and its staff have to try harder than the conventional college. Even when students want to and perhaps feel they do belong, the external facade of a large and complex organization can present a daunting aspect to those who visit it infrequently.

> I feel myself belonging to the Polytechnic but I don't feel the Polytechnic considers me as part of it. (Hong Kong–Student Guidance)

A sense of belonging can be developed, though.

> Having being a distance learning student in the Hong Kong Polytechnic for nearly 3 years now, I have a deep feeling that I belong to this institution. (Hong Kong–Textiles)

To establish collective affiliation there needs to be a sufficient level of contact and communication between the students and the college. Taylor *et al.* (1986) thought that their multi-institutional study provided some evidence that increased contact between institution and student increased integration and hence persistence. However, as they caution, the data was not easy to interpret, since persisting students have greater opportunities for contact.

The human contact of the academic support system provides a clear opportunity for enhancing collective affiliation. Collective affiliation is more likely to result if tutors devote their time to tutoring and counseling, rather than to alternative programs devoted solely to socialization. Kember and Dekkers (1987, pp. 9-11) found that students placed limited value on social functions with either fellow students or academic staff. Friendships can develop, but more through collective study experiences than events specifically devoted to socializing.

Communication Channels

Collective affiliation between student and institution can be enhanced through any of the channels of communication between the two. Each of the sectors of a college can communicate with students through a variety of media channels, such as telephone, mail, electronic mail, video link or direct face-to-face contact.

Mail

Mail is commonly used for students to submit assignments and for tutors to return them with marks and comments. Mail can in addition be used for individual counseling and for other interaction between college and student or vice versa. Whether interaction by mail can contribute to collective affiliation is more questionable.

Bååth (1980) made an extensive empirical investigation of postal two-way communication in correspondence education, though did not directly investigate the posed question. The studied variable closest to degree of interaction was density of submitted assignments. In all courses greater density of submissions correlated with higher levels of students completing the course. However, this was probably a trivial finding since greater assignment density corresponds with earlier assignments, which inevitably means more students still doing the course at that stage. The more important finding was that there was no overall significant correlation between submission density and persistence. The results also suggest that it was possible to replace substantial numbers of assignment questions by self-assessment questions without any noticeable effect on the students.

The Bååth study therefore appears to provide no positive evidence to suggest that collective affiliation can be built up by mail correspondence. Intuitively mail seems unlikely to be a highly effective medium for building collective affiliation.

Telephone

Williams and Chapanis (1976) compared face-to-face and telephone communication, and found that either medium was as effective for tasks such as exchanging information or opinions, asking questions or solving problems. For tasks such as persuasion or establishing relationships, face-to-face contact was more effective. Research into tutorials at the Open University of the United Kingdom suggested that telephone tutorials were found to be more task efficient but more formal and less spontaneous than face-to-face meetings (Rutter & Robinson, 1981).

Flinck (1978) reported an experiment in which students received tutor initiated telephone calls. The majority of the students receiving calls expressed a positive reaction, with only a very small proportion of students having a negative reaction. Further, 61% of the students had introduced topics of a personal or social nature into the conversation, which tutors initially related to submitted assignments. This study provides clear evidence that tutor initiated telephone tutoring can contribute to collective affiliation.

If calls initiated by tutors can have this positive effect then surely student initiated calls must also have potential for building collective affiliation. For the students to experience a positive feeling, they must either be able to get straight through to their tutor or have their call returned quickly. Advertised availability times, direct dial facilities, recorded answer-phone services and access to home numbers can all help in this respect.

Face-to-face Contact

The comparison of telephone and face-to-face contact above implies that face-to-face contact should be better for establishing relationships than telephone communications. In our Hong Kong study (Kember, Lai, Murphy, Siaw & Yuen, 1992c) only one student expressed a preference for contact with tutors via telephone counseling as it generated a faster response. The remaining interviewees preferred direct face-to-face contact with the tutors.

At first sight, therefore, face-to-face meetings at tutorials or residential schools would appear to be most effective at building collective affiliation. However, the provision of local tutorials is expensive, and difficult to organize if students are dispersed. For the cost of one face-to-face tutorial it may be possible to provide several teleconference tutorials accessible by a far wider range of students. As the telephone appears to be as effective a medium for the normal content of a tutorial, once the cost equation is taken into account, the teleconference tutorial may become more effective at building collective affiliation than the face-to-face tutorial.

The student side must also be taken into account. Many students enroll in open learning courses because they are unable or unwilling to attend regular classes on campus. This does not necessarily imply that they do not wish to have any classes, but it does mean that tutorials should be at convenient times and places and the duration of classes should not be excessive.

Residential schools provide a good opportunity for enhancing collective affiliation. However, they can have a negative effect on social and family integration. A student who uses a holiday period and goes to some expense to attend a residential school, leaving the spouse in charge of the children, is contributing little to family harmony. Residential schools are, therefore, seen as contributing to collective affiliation, but should be voluntary, unless they include a component which is absolutely impossible to provide at a distance. Generation of collective affiliation does not justify residential schools for all students or all courses irrespective of their nature.

Administrative Support

The discussion and the research studies cited above have concentrated on contact between tutors or faculty members and students. Those who operate administrative support systems can also contribute to collective affiliation in either positive or negative ways. An efficient service with speedy attention to queries creates the impression that the student is dealing with a responsive professional organization. Unfortunately, it only takes one or two foul-ups to destroy a good impression created over a period of time.

The model offers neither a simple blueprint for the creation of an efficient organization nor a magic formula for the elimination of foul-ups. If any administrative policy is more likely to enhance collective affiliation, it may be that of localization. Students are more likely to associate with the human presence of a local liaison officer or study center facilitator than with an apparently impersonal central bureaucracy. As it would be difficult to devolve full administrative responsibility, the role of the local administrator is often that of interpreting and explaining administrative requirements to the student. Should satisfaction not be achieved the local administrator can intercede with the central bureaucracy on behalf of the student. Various administrative systems with an element of localization are described by Livingston (1985), Store and Chick (1984), Timmins (1986), Walker (1982) and Waqa (1984).

Group or Individual Contact

Another dimension to the provision of academic support is whether students receive individual communications or whether some element of group activity takes place. In many instances this choice will be somewhat constrained by logistical considerations, in particular by the distribution of students. Group activity, though, does not have to mean that participants are all together in the same physical location. By using a teleconference or video link it is possible for widely distributed students to enjoy most of the benefits of group activity (e.g., Jaques, 1984) from their own homes or a nearby study center.

If group activity, whether face-to-face or through telecommunication media, is possible it is then necessary to consider whether it is desirable. Students usually choose open learning because they are unable to study full-time due to work and/or family commitments. This choice, though, does not normally imply that the students are unable or unwilling to attend any classes, but it does suggest that meetings should not be too frequent and should be at convenient times and places.

Groups of distance learners have been identified who have chosen the mode because they dislike or perceive no need for contact with other students, or meetings with tutors (Thorpe, 1987). Such students normally seem to be a very small minority, however. Thorpe *et al.* (1986) report that less than ten percent of a large sample of students of the Open University of the United Kingdom reported no direct contact with tutors or other students. Even that small percentage would have contained many who could not, rather than did not, want to make contact. In the Hong Kong study (Kember, Lai, Murphy, Siaw & Yuen, 1992c) no evidence of any students who wished to study in isolation could be found among those interviewed. The majority of the students expressed a preference for meetings with the tutor to be as a group rather than as a one-to-one counseling session if that were possible.

> I prefer face-to-face classes because I will be able to listen to other students' problems. (Hong Kong–OLIHK)

Not only was there no evidence of students wishing to study in isolation but there seemed to be marked ambivalence concerning mode of study. When asked which mode of study they would prefer, the responses were about evenly divided between full-time, part-time and distance learning. Many replies were couched with riders or conditions.

> Full time is not possible. I will choose part-time if the number of lectures does not exceed twice per week, otherwise I will choose distance learning which will save me a lot of traveling time to the Polytechnic. (Hong Kong–Student Guidance)

In summary, distance education courses inevitably have less class contact than full-time courses. This does not imply that those who enroll in such courses want no classes at all. In fact quite the contrary, the available evidence suggests that many students perceive benefits from some level of contact, and what is more these benefits are usually realized.

Group Activities

In the Hong Kong study, all of the courses examined took advantage of the concentrated population to offer face-to-face sessions at a frequency greater than most comparable courses elsewhere. Two courses included group activities as an integral feature of the course design in a way which is quite unusual for distance learning courses.

The course in student guidance recognized the value of group sessions in achieving objectives relating to counseling skills, group dynamics and group-work strategies. A series of colloquia and workshops was therefore planned as an integral part of the course. The assessment for the course consisted of group and individual project work, the outcomes of which were presented at colloquia. During the first semester of the course there were six colloquia, each lasting for a Saturday morning, which the students were required to attend. In addition there were optional tutorials for guidance on project work and presentation, and help with study problems.

Some students did not find the optional tutorials particularly useful, but the colloquia and workshops were very well received.

> I attend all of them. They are quite helpful. At the meetings, I learn through communication with other classmates. My point of view is thus broadened. (Hong Kong–Student Guidance)

> Since the tutorial is optional, I will not attend if it is unnecessary. Only students who are going to present in the next colloquium will attend the tutorial. In fact I come back just to listen to other students' queries about the course. It seems to me that its function is to prepare those students who are going to present in the following week. Most of the time is spent discussing what to do in the colloquium. (Hong Kong–Student Guidance)

> They are helpful to me. Doing a workshop is much better than just reading the theories in books. Workshops are especially good for in-service teachers since most of the theories have been studied in our Certificate of Education. (Hong Kong–Student Guidance)

The quotations reveal that not only are the meetings valued by the students, but also the objectives related to group communication are being achieved.

The education degree course placed great value on group work, and built in requirements for such work within the course materials. Students were placed, or placed themselves, in a "group of five," each of which might actually contain between three and seven people, depending on logistics and student distribution. A significant proportion of the activities within the course materials required each student to make use of the "group of five." For example, one activity involved the taking of photographs of the students (who were all practicing teachers) in their normal classroom setting. The photographs would then be passed to other group members who would make written comments. The photographs and the comments would ultimately form part of submitted assignment work.

Students found such work helped their study, helped to build confidence and was an enjoyable experience.

> Yes, the 'group of 5' has helped me in doing the tasks. My personal thinking about the idea cannot guarantee whether I am right. Listening to other classmates' ideas gives me more confidence as to whether my ideas are right or wrong. (Hong Kong–Education)

> Our group has helped me with the tasks. In fact we help each other to solve any problems. Our group is running quite well, sometimes our discussion can even last seven hours. It is worthwhile to have the study group because it is a very effective method in our learning process. (Hong Kong–Education)

It is instructive to note that both the student guidance and the education degree courses had drop-out rates below ten percent, which is remarkably low for open learning courses. While not claiming that the group work wholly accounted for this phenomenon, it would seem to be a strongly contributing factor towards persistence in the courses.

In view of the popularity of the groups of five in the education course, effort might profitably be directed towards assisting students to organize self-study groups in other courses. Merely issuing students with a list of other students' addresses, as commonly happens, usually seems to achieve very little. Self-study groups are more likely to be successful if, as in the education course, the course design incorporates activities suitable for group interaction, as advocated and described in Kember and Murphy (1994). There are a variety of ways in which peer tutoring has been utilized in classroom education (see, e.g.,

Goldschmid & Goldschmid, 1976; Goodlad & Hirst, 1989) which have not been widely explored in distance education.

Human Contact in Distance Education

Discussion of the role of group activities is part of a wider debate on the place of human contact in distance education. Views which have been expressed can be placed on a spectrum from those who believe in the desirability of levels of contact approaching those of classroom-based education to advocates of the complete absence of any contact. Views towards the no contact end of the spectrum were advanced in a paper titled, "Is any face-to-face contact necessary in distance education?" by Taylor and White (1981). They suggested that cognitive objectives do not necessarily demand face-to-face contact and that a large proportion of courses they examined contained only cognitive objectives. They noted, however, that many of these courses did have residential schools or other forms of contact so drew the following conclusion.

> Perhaps, the resources allocated to these activities could be better spent on the development of instructional strategies designed specifically to promote the achievement of objectives in the cognitive domain. None of these strategies necessarily demand face-to-face contact. (Taylor & White, 1981, pp. 7-8)

Sewart (1981) advanced an alternative position by arguing that the human element had an important role to play in adapting the study package to the almost infinite variety of student needs. He argued that it was inefficient, if not impossible, for a study package to cater for the learning needs of all students, particularly as adult learners tend to be heterogeneous. In Smith and Kelly (1987) it is argued that there is a trend towards the convergence of distance and mainstream education. Where this is happening mainstream education makes more use of learning resources and distance education incorporates higher levels of interaction. Clearly if this trend is to progress then the levels of human contact in distance education courses will increase. Many open learning courses already make use of study packages in the context of a supported study group.

The model offers clear backing for the incorporation of greater levels of group activity within open learning courses. Participation in group activities can have a marked contribution

to enhancing collective affiliation as well as bringing other
educational benefits (Jaques, 1984).

Normative Congruence

The model stresses the importance of integration with the
academic environment. The normative congruence facet of this
integration component, calls for compatibility between the
academic expectations of faculty and the students' image of
those expectations. Integration will therefore not occur when the
student is unaware of an academic convention or has a different
perception of a task, or an alternative conception of knowledge,
to faculty. Academics have expectations of student performance
and conventions which students are supposed to follow. The
type of performance demanded and the academic conventions
are often quite different to superficially similar expectations met
previously by new students at school or in the workplace.

Many students new to open learning are therefore faced with the
need to learn new conventions and recognize quite different
conceptions of knowledge. Some unfortunately fail to realize that
any reorientation is necessary so never integrate with the norms of
academic study. The model suggests that they drop-out. Others
realize that new conventions need to be adopted and skills
acquired but find the process difficult. Unlearning a pattern of
behavior to replace it with another is never an easy process. In
this case it is particularly difficult, since many academics find it
difficult to define or articulate their performance expectations
and the skills of their disciplines.

> Yes, I felt discouraged and frustrated and often came close to
> giving up when I worked on my first assignment. Luckily the
> support from my group kept me in the course. I knew that I wasn't
> the only person to have problems with the first assignment, there
> were the same problems faced by my group mates as well. Now, I
> do not have the feeling of giving up since I understand its learning
> approach–free thinking. (Hong Kong–Education)

There is empirical evidence for the contention that normative
congruence in the academic sphere influences student progress.
Kember and Harper (1987) used discriminant analysis to relate
drop-out to demographic variables and a number of scales
related to approaches to studying. The variable which best
distinguished between drop-outs and course completers was that

of surface approach. In terms of the model, students who habitually employed a surface approach were unable to integrate with the more complex learning approaches consistent with the aims of higher education.

In achieving normative congruence, or in this instance achieving compatibility between course demands and student learning approaches, two issues need to be addressed. Firstly students who would normally make appropriate use of the deep approach but, because of factors such as surface assessment demands, high workloads, over-prescriptive courses or an inhospitable learning environment, resort to a surface approach. This problem can be ameliorated only if the factors influencing students towards a surface approach are addressed by curriculum design, instructional design or institutional policy. This was the topic of the previous chapter–designing instruction so as to encourage students to employ a deep rather than a surface approach to learning.

It should be noted that offering study skills programs to reorient students towards a deep approach, as discussed below, will achieve nothing if the course the students are to study makes surface demands. Contrary to what might or ought to be expected, all too many courses in higher education inadvertently encourage students to employ a surface approach. There is now such extensive evidence of student use of surface approaches increasing through a course, that it has unfortunately become a norm to expect this pattern (e.g., Biggs, 1987; Gow & Kember, 1990; Watkins & Hattie, 1985). There often appears to be a mismatch between espoused theory and theory in practice (Argyris & Schön, 1978). Colleges espouse goals such as the development of the ability to solve novel problems or critical thinking, but in practice devise courses which largely test students' ability to reproduce bodies of knowledge presented by the faculty.

The quantitative tests of the model provided further evidence of colleges failing to reward students who employ a deep approach. In neither the original test nor the replication study was there a significant path between the academic integration factor and either GPA or drop-out ratio. The disturbing explanation for these concurring results is that the courses' assessment processes did not really test for or encourage the desirable learning qualities encapsulated in the deep approach and intrinsic motivation subscales which are part of the academic integration construct.

Reorienting students towards the use of a deep approach will achieve little in such a learning environment, since students will soon perceive that the course does not require a deep approach and switch back to a surface approach. Students who are able to employ a deep approach will still employ a surface approach if a deep approach does not seem to be demanded, goes unrewarded or is difficult to achieve in a hostile learning environment.

Reorienting Approaches to Learning

There are students who habitually employ a surface approach to study in courses which do anticipate a deep approach and do have a learning environment appropriate for meaningful learning. Such students need assistance to develop the capability of appropriately utilizing a deep approach. The most common reason for students to employ inappropriate learning approaches in a favorable context is that their conception of knowledge or the requirements of academic study is not consistent with the conventional requirements of academe (Marton, Dall'Alba & Beaty, 1993). The primary concern of any learning skills program should, therefore, be the reorientation of students' conceptions of knowledge.

The conventional answer to such problems has been the offering of courses with titles such as study skills or learning skills programs. There has been considerable debate about both the effectiveness of and a suitable form for such initiatives. The protagonists in the debate are still far from agreement on many issues. This chapter cannot hope to summarize much less resolve the areas of contention. Instead I will attempt to draw upon this literature, from the perspective of the model of student progress, taking particular cognizance of the open learning context.

Many traditional study skills courses may be positively harmful as they commonly contain sections on enhancing memorization by techniques like rehearsal or mnemonics. Hypothetical graphs, showing memory decay with time, are used to reinforce the exhortations to constantly revise the material presented. Study skills programs with this type of content surely would tend to reinforce the notion that rote learning is appropriate. Gibbs (1981, p. 61) has produced a damning critique of such study skills courses which not only castigates proponents for these likely negative effects but also exposes the shallow research from which the memorization techniques are derived.

Study skills courses can have the opposite effect to that intended. Ramsden, Beswick and Bowden (1986), for example, reported a study skills course which was designed with the intention of encouraging meaningful approaches to learning. However, the program in which the students were enrolled gave the impression that the opposite approach was rewarded. As a result students took from the study skills course only those skills they thought would be useful in their wider program, which to them seemed to require atomistic items of knowledge to be remembered and reproduced in examinations. The outcome was that use of a surface approach went up rather than down following the introduction of the study skills course. The students simply became better at doing what they thought the program required.

Alternatives to traditional study skills programs are the metacognitive approaches to assisting students with their learning approaches, which have been reviewed by Ford (1981). Baird and White (1982) assert that learning will be improved if the learners are trained in processes of self-evaluation and decision making so that they can be aware of the process and nature of their learning. Others (e.g., Martin & Ramsden, 1987) have advocated courses which encourage students to reflect upon their own learning. Evidence that programs can encourage the use of a deep approach through self-reflection on learning comes from Dart and Clarke (1991) and Davies, Sivan and Kember (in press).

Gibbs (1981) maintains that it is necessary to spend a period of time actively examining both the content and processes of their learning. The Gibbs' method is based on structured discussions. Typically a topic of specific relevance to the students' course is chosen and students are first asked to individually reflect on their approach to such tasks. Pairs of students might then compare perceptions before a wider discussion within a group of four. In the final plenary session the outcomes of the discussion groups would be drawn together. The role of the tutor is to facilitate and structure the discussion, rather than to teach. Outcomes and skills are not prescribed.

Direct adoption of these procedures for distance education courses is clearly difficult. Students could be given the original discussion material for the exercises in their study guides or in an ancillary booklet. For example, Gibbs (1984, p. 276) shows two student essays which are to be compared. Some of the smaller group discussions could no doubt be replaced by either conversational style comments from a tutor or a taped conversation between students. Discussion could be provided at tutorials or by teleconference. Modification of the procedure would involve some compromise between the structure of the discussion method (Northedge, 1975) and the imposition of constraints on study time and location for the part-time student, who may have chosen the mode to be free of such constraints.

Kirkup (1984) has described an alternative type of program, which was devised specifically for an open learning course. The course integrated "study notes" with the main content of the technology course. The study notes aimed to develop the studying and writing skills of the students, but were not intended to be prescriptive. Rather they encouraged students to reflect on their purposes for studying and to select appropriate methods for achieving their purpose.

This course can be seen as adopting a middle ground between two paradigms for study skills courses described by Taylor (1984). It differs from "study methods courses" in that the study notes are placed in the context of the body of content for the course. Exercises are designed to both develop learning skills and to relate to the course objectives. It avoids being prescriptive by offering students a range of techniques. Finally, from Kirkup's (1984) description, it at least tried to orient students towards a deep approach by adopting a metacognitive outlook.

The approach of integrating study notes into open learning courses has not been widely adopted. One obvious reason is that considerable resources are needed to develop such courses. It is significant that the course described by Kirkup (1984) is one of a limited number of foundation courses which would be taken by students involved in diverse programs. One of few other colleges which has also developed courses with integrated study skills components is Murdoch University in Australia, which also has multi-disciplinary foundation courses. If there are only a limited number of foundation or entry courses available, then few courses need the infusion of study skills advice. Also, common foundation courses imply large student numbers which helps to justify the extra resources.

It would be fruitless to recommend that all units taken by first-year students be redeveloped with an integrated study skills approach, similar to that described by Kirkup (1984), since resources are unlikely to be made available for such a large project. Recommending the adoption of common foundation courses to justify integrated study skills courses is even more pointless. In the unlikely event that the faculty could be persuaded to accept such a change, the resources needed to restructure the courses would be even greater than those needed to develop integrated study skills materials. Common foundation courses may also be incompatible with the development of intrinsic motivation, since students might well end up taking courses unrelated to their specific interests.

There are, therefore, difficulties in implementing Gibbs' style workshops for distance education courses, and extensive resource requirements for fully integrated courses. The next part of this discussion explores the possibility of study skills initiatives which draw elements from the discussed programs, but require reasonable resources, and which are practicable in the distance education context.

First, examining the integrated approach, the resource barrier is the need to develop integrated material for each course, at least at the introductory level. There is a possibility for compromise if the material consists of sections drawn from a bank of general study skills advice, together with exercises related to the specific course.

The general bank of advice might include reading skills, such as locating main ideas, recognizing organizational patterns, reading for inference, summarizing texts and questioning, together with planning, researching and organizing essays. With such material the traps are to avoid being over-prescriptive, to steer clear of any recommendations which might reinforce or encourage rote-learning, and to avoid recommending time consuming practices that even the writers do not follow.

Activities for the study skills material should, as far as possible, utilize material from the content of the course. Reading exercises should concentrate on set articles or the course text books. Howard (1985) has described the use of audio tapes designed to accompany course readings, mainly in the form of modeled self-instruction or dialogue with one's self. Marshall (1984) described audio tapes which are content related and incorporate the principles of peer learning. Using audio tapes would be a comparatively low cost way of focusing general study skills advice towards specific reading and writing exercises.

Audio tapes could also mimic to some extent the type of discussion which would take place in a Gibbs' style workshop. Marshall's tapes appear to have been influenced by Gibbs' ideas. The simulated discussions on audio tapes could be reinforced with a limited number of group discussions at study centers, residential schools or by teleconference.

Summary and Preview

The chapter has considered academic support services in terms of the two integration facets of Durkheim's theory of suicide, namely collective affiliation and normative congruence. Collective affiliation can be developed by students experiencing positive reactions to contact with faculty and administrative support staff. Unfortunately, it is also all too easy for students to develop a sense of disenchantment from contact with cold, unhelpful or bureaucratic personnel.

The nature of the communication channel will influence the degree to which the establishment of collective affiliation is likely. Direct human contact seems to be the ideal for building relationships. The more closely a communication channel relates to direct contact the easier it is likely to be to develop affinity. There is also some evidence that group contact is better than individual for developing collective affiliation as there is the possibility of student-student interaction as well as student-faculty.

A major reason for drop-out can be lack of normative congruence between students' conceptions of study or knowledge and academic requirements. Academic support to students might, therefore, focus upon reorienting students conceptions of academic demands. The chapter has discussed possible formats for such academic support at some length.

As adult students are heterogeneous, an element of individual counseling to assist with specific study problems would be advantageous. The nature of this counseling or tutoring and the type of person to provide it, is discussed in the next chapter. The personnel aspects of both tutoring and administrative support are discussed further in Chapter 15. The final part of Chapter 15 takes the opportunity to examine the support provision with respect to both academic and social integration.

Chapter 15

Counseling for Social Integration

Synopsis

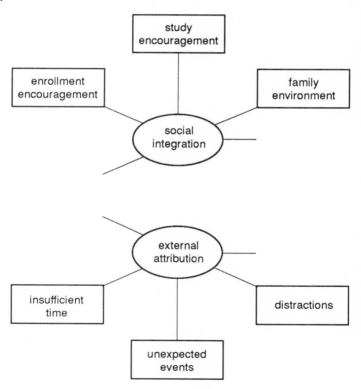

The model provides support to open access policies because it shows that entry characteristics have little direct influence on student progress in part-time courses for adults. The students' background does, though, influence the difficulties which have to be overcome if social integration is to be successful. The model provides a framework for counseling students in anticipating and overcoming social integration demands.

The model provides a preview of difficulties students are likely to face. It can, therefore, serve as the foundation for pre-enrollment counseling packages or meetings which aim to forewarn students of potential difficulties they may face and decisions which will have to be made. The need to integrate study with existing commitments can be highlighted and students asked to devise plans to cope with this necessity.

The model also provides a rationale for counseling students who fall behind once the course is under way. Comparison between the social integration and external integration elements of the model suggests that counselors stress the importance of students accepting responsibility for their own progress rather than blaming external factors. The social integration component suggests areas which may need discussion if students are to cope with a course.

Social Integration or External Attribution?

Students entering open learning courses can take the track towards integrating academic requirements with work, family and social demands. Those who do not proceed on this track start blaming factors apparently beyond their control for their lack of progress as an open learning student. Clearly it is in the interest of all concerned if the students take the former track.

Few, though, would underestimate the implications of this statement. The most widely adopted criterion of open learning courses is probably an open access policy. Students admitted to open learning courses may not have the academic qualifications expected of those who enter college direct from high school. They might have had little or no contact with an academic environment so be unused to the expectations and the, often implicit, conventions of academe. It is quite probable that new students will never before have had to fit study demands into their schedule of work and family commitments. In making this adjustment some may get little help from workmates, family or friends. Some may even face antagonism.

Not all students, of course, face this daunting array of hurdles. Because of past education, previous experience or a more supportive environment many have a smoother path. It should also be prominently noted that one of the most satisfying aspects for those involved in open learning courses for adults is that students can and do overcome extreme disadvantages to go on to complete courses.

Who Is Responsible?

Given that some students can succeed from initial positions which appear disadvantageous, it can be tempting to leave success or failure entirely to the students. It is a common attitude among faculty that their role is to teach (or lecture) and it is up to the students as to whether or not they learn. Failures to learn are ascribed to students lacking motivation or not being of adequate quality for the course.

There are two main arguments against this attitude. The first is research which indicates that faculty who hold such conceptions of teaching and learning tend to be associated with courses which discourage meaningful approaches to learning or have a negative influence on the quality of learning (Gow & Kember, 1993; Kember & Gow, 1994). More successful teachers are those who see their role as encompassing motivation and learning facilitation and who take a pastoral interest in their students. The other argument is to point to the influence of pre-enrollment or new student support programs. Clearly these are not always successful, but there is sufficient evidence of their contributing to successful student outcomes (e.g., Bowser & Race, 1991; Kember, 1982; Zajkowski, 1993) to show that students can and should be provided with advice and assistance.

The very existence of special programs or people appointed to a counseling role can, though, serve to minimize the involvement in a counseling role of others who have contact with students. If student counselors do exist, then it could be a reasonable reaction to leave or refer all pastoral issues to those qualified for or appointed to a counseling role. Faculty may interpret their role as confined to teaching their own course and not feel it necessary to advise on study techniques or inquire about social integration issues. Those involved in enrolling students might envisage this as a purely administrative process devoid of any requirement to advise or welcome students.

I believe that all members of a college who have any direct or indirect contact with students will play a part in developing students' level of collective affiliation towards the institution. Warmth, interest and perceived competence will contribute towards a sense of belonging. Coolness, tardiness in responding, bureaucratic indifference and incompetence will all have a negative impact which is often not perceived by those responsible for engendering it.

I go further to assert that, not only can all college staff contribute to developing or destroying collective affiliation, but also all who have contact with students should see their role as encompassing some element of counseling and advising students. For most it need not be a major role but all persons the students have contact with should at least show interest and concern for them.

The reason for not abdicating responsibility to counselors is quite simply that part-time students, particularly those at a distance, are unlikely to make contact with a counselor. For full-time on-campus students, withdrawal is a process requiring formal decisions and positive actions. College authorities have to be notified of withdrawal from courses and that the student is vacating accommodation. When a student initiates the formal withdrawal process, if not before, there can be time for referral to a counselor, who is normally on-hand.

By contrast, it is easy for part-time students to cease working on a course without informing anyone at all. When students find a course difficult or do not make sufficient time available for study, they can simply decide to cease working on the course. It is all too easy for students to gradually drift into this situation by progressively falling behind schedule and eventually feel that they cannot meet assignment deadliness. While this process is happening, though, there is little incentive to contact a counselor. It would seem to some to be an admission of failure. Others might perceive that there would be little that a counselor could do to help. Whatever their perception of the value of counseling, there can be little incentive to contact a name in a telephone directory, who might well be based at a distant campus.

As part-time students, particularly those at a distance, tend not to initiate contact when at risk, all faculty and administrators who do come into contact with students should be prepared to go beyond a narrow interpretation of their role. Even a few friendly words can mean that students will be prepared to contact a person if at some later date they need advice.

Some staff happily accept a pastoral approach towards students with little or no prompting. In other cases attitudes need to be changed or developed. Attitude change is often a difficult process, but in this instance the process can be aided by a workshop which aims to make staff more aware of the apprehensions of new students and the problems they face. Students, themselves, could be invited to talk to groups of staff. Staff might then discuss ways in which they can help alleviate these student concerns.

It is often not easy for faculty to form warm relationships with students because of the physical distance between them and the limited opportunities for contact.

> I have no comment on the tutors' characters since I seldom make contact with them. (Hong Kong–Textiles)

Some students can also be suspicious of contact with faculty. Those charged with their education in the past, such as high school teachers, may well have acted in an authoritative distant manner.

> Definitely there is a distance between the distance learner and the tutors, and it is very big. It all depends on tutors, of how they handle the case, some tutors are friendly and easy to deal with but they are only a minor group. My experience tells me that most of the people are not nice. Man is man, we always try to keep our distance. (Hong Kong–Textiles)

The contrasting quotations below show that whether empathy develops between tutor and student depends very much on the manner displayed by the tutor.

> I find that the tutors are friendly and easy to deal with. (Hong Kong–Textiles)

> The tutor for Business Communication was fierce and tough. During the tutorial periods, he/she would keep on asking students until he/she obtained a satisfactory answer. Sometimes it was really embarrassing to students; whereas the tutor for Management was friendly. (Hong Kong–OLIHK)

Proactive Rather Than Reactive

Given that distance education students can be reluctant to contact a tutor, some colleges have instituted policies for tutors to initiate contact with students. Typically a tutor will make an introductory telephone call to all new students, or to any not attending tutorials, or those who are late with assignments.

There is some evidence that the higher levels of contact between the student and the institution is associated with greater persistence. There can be difficulties in interpreting the data from studies of this type, though, since those who persist longer with a course inevitably have a greater period and more opportunities for making contacts. Any attempt to control for the opportunity period is bound to be highly arbitrary as institutions rarely know how long students remain genuinely active on a course.

The relationship between persistence and various types of student contact has been examined by several research teams in a variety of contexts. Rekkedal (1973) conducted an experiment with the turn-around time of assignments. The experiment suggested that drop-out rates might be reduced if assignment turn-around was faster. Taylor *et al.* (1986) questioned the general applicability of Rekkedal's work, so conducted a much more extensive investigation involving five institutions in four countries. They discovered no significant relationship between turn-around time and persistence. Two of the four institutions with sufficient data showed significant relationships between feedback interval and persistence. The data on additional contacts besides those related to assignments needed to be interpreted cautiously because of the inherent problem noted above. Taylor *et al.* believed, though, that their data were generally supportive of the assertion that additional contacts with students can lead to greater student retention.

Flink (1978) conducted an experiment with tutor-initiated telephone tutoring. Students experiencing the telephone tutoring performed better in the final test than the control group. Scales (1984) reported a modest, but statistically significant, relationship between the number of telephone contacts and persistence in a study at the Open Learning Institute in British Columbia. The relationship was stronger for student-initiated calls than for tutor-initiated calls.

Some of the research on student contact and persistence is inconclusive. Where relationships have been observed, they have consistently been in a positive direction. I have been unable to find anything other than isolated individual instances of student-tutor contact having a negative effect on student persistence. The most plausible conclusion is that increasing the levels of tutor-student contact does increase completion rates, though the effect is probably small.

This conclusion can be interpreted as supporting the model proposed in this book. The model suggests that student progress can be enhanced by tutor-student contact, as it can contribute to enhancing collective affiliation, and advice can help students with both social and academic integration. The experimental data are, therefore, quite consistent with the predictions of the model. It should also encourage colleges to introduce schemes whereby their faculty and support staff do initiate contact with students.

The Student Side

Colleges can enhance student progress by encouraging their staff to initiate contact with students. Enhanced contacts, though, do not diminish the obligation upon the students to adopt appropriate attitudes and to take responsibility for their own learning outcomes.

Students who do not accept responsibility for their own progression attribute lack of progress to factors outside their control. Chapter 8 is replete with quotations from students who blame everything and everyone from demanding employers, through troublesome children, to desirable social acquaintances, for their failure to complete courses. It is certainly true that part-time study is difficult because of these conflicting obligations. There are also part-time students, though, who face these daunting commitments but are able to integrate them with the additional requirements of part-time study.

The model suggests that those who continue to externalize responsibility for learning outcomes will not progress. Those who accept responsibility for their own progress are on the positive track to success.

Realistic Expectations

One of the most common contributing factors to students failing
to assimilate with academic expectations or integrating study
with social obligations is that their expectations were not
realistic. Abel (1966), Kearney (1969) and Knoell (1966) have all
found evidence of higher drop-out rates among students with
unrealistic goals. Students with little or no experience of
education beyond high school can have little insight into the
expectations and conventions of academe. There may well be no
history of study or even serious reading within their family life. It
is difficult for such students to visualize the requirements of part-
time study.

> Before starting the course, I thought it would be very easy and I
> wouldn't need to spend much time on it. But now as the exam is
> approaching, I have worries and am less confident about it. I
> intend to repeat the course. (Hong Kong–Taxation)

Even students who have completed college degrees as full-time
students can be taken aback by the different demands of part-
time study. The following student was in a post-graduate course
so would be well versed in the ways of academe.

> I was not well informed about the details of the course. At the
> very beginning I misunderstood the meaning of distance education.
> As mentioned earlier, I thought that it was similar to a
> correspondence course. I assumed that the class met only twice a
> term. I also misunderstood the frequency of the assignments. I
> thought at most there would be one assignment only for each
> subject, but later it was found that there were two assignments for
> each subject and participation in the colloquium. (Hong Kong–
> Student Guidance)

There are programs which aim to provide potential or new
students with a more realistic insight into academic life. One
simple procedure is to suggest that potential students think about
their current timetable or schedule and try to see where a realistic
period of study can be accommodated.

Zajkowski (1993) pilot tested the use of a pre-enrollment
counseling booklet which invited prospective students to consider
their aims, motivation and preparedness for academic study. In
the subsequent course, completion rates were twice as high for
those completing the booklet as for a control group. There was

also some indication that the booklets were effective in self-selection during the pre-enrollment period.

A very realistic way to gain experience of academic expectations is through a trial course. The Open University of the United Kingdom counts the first three months of all courses as a trial period (McIntosh, Woodley & Morrison, 1980). Students do not formally enroll and pay the substantial part of the course fee until the end of the trial period.

These trial periods mean that new students are taking the normal courses. There are also special programs for new students. An integrated learning skills program (Kirkup, 1984) was discussed in the last chapter. Study notes were integrated with the normal content of the course. Bowser and Race (1991) describe a short orientation program for new students held in local study centers.

It would be useful to have longitudinal studies of such programs to see how effective they are in facilitating entry into normal courses. Such studies should try to answer the difficult question of whether those who do successfully proceed to complete a subsequent course would have been able to do so irrespective of the introductory program. What is clear is that the duration of introductory programs should be kept as brief as possible. Students facing a part-time college course which can last for seven or eight years do not want that period significantly lengthened.

Realistic Information

Another way in which colleges can help prepare students for the demands of part-time study is by providing realistic and accurate information about course expectations and the time needed to complete courses. Unfortunately, advertising and course prospectuses are normally designed to entice students to enroll rather than to warn them of the obligations and demands of academic study. Governments increasingly expect colleges to behave in an entrepreneurial manner and increase student numbers. Part-time open learning students can be one of few potential markets in which expansion is possible.

Because courses can be offered at a distance, colleges are not confined to recruiting in their local area. This statement is particularly striking from a Hong Kong perspective. Courses are offered by institutions based in Australia, Britain, Canada, Hong Kong, Macau, New Zealand, the USA, and probably a few more countries besides. The Hong Kong Council for Academic Accreditation was reported (Lee, 1993) as having found at least 153 distance learning courses advertised in the territory in a period of less than a year. As many courses did not need to be registered with the authority, the only way they had to find out that such courses were offered was by spotting an advertisement. The figure given is, therefore, probably a significant underestimate.

Students may not always be faced with so many institutions competing to enroll them and take their fee payment, but in most countries students do have a range of options if they wish to enroll in an open learning course. Given this level of competition, it is almost inevitable that advertising concentrates upon the rewards which can accrue from obtaining an award rather than the study obligations. Advertisements often state that "programs can be completed in as little as X years." It may only be after the fee is paid that the student realizes that the program can be completed in X years for those granted maximum exemptions, and if they take twice the normal load, but average completion times might be considerably longer.

In an environment which links institutions' budgets to student numbers, and results in commissions paid for students recruited, it is difficult to envisage greater frankness in course advertising. This is particularly true for the recruiting of international students because the level of control and regulation is often less than an institution would experience in its own country. Students can find themselves committed to a course before they realize the extent of the demands of part-time study. The following two quotations are from a student enrolled in one of the courses in Hong Kong.

> The course is very hard for me. I really don't like the course. When the course started, I just realized that it is distance learning which I am most afraid of. I am a person who likes to receive the conventional type of learning. Now I have to depend on myself for everything and I overestimated my English ability. Since I have paid the school fees, I can't withdraw voluntarily and I am waiting to be failed by Deakin University. What I really want to say is that this course is very hard for me and it is beyond my capability of reading those materials. I sacrificed all my social life and rest time which makes me unhappy. I feel very

discouraged from doing the course. I must admit that I have made a wrong decision.

I feel very discouraged from doing this course. I feel very sorry about the school fee of $HK 20, 000 (about $US 2, 600) so am not giving up this course yet. If the school fee was refundable I would give up the course right away. (Hong Kong–Education)

The college which enrolled him was one which provided local support so there would have been people at hand to discuss course requirements. There are presumably many more students in this predicament after enrolling with institutions offering less support, or none at all.

Course prospectuses and advertising are unlikely to become more realistic while institutions remain under pressure to recruit extra students. Where government funding is involved, one solution could be to relate budgets to numbers of graduates rather than numbers enrolled on a course, as usually seems to be the case. Such a move might herald a quite different attitude among colleges, but would need to be applied carefully as it might discourage recruitment of students from disadvantaged situations.

Tutoring, Counseling and Supporting Students

Several previous sections have referred to roles for institutional staff in various types of student support. This section attempts to draw together several aspects of the role of support staff. It discusses the range of functions to be performed, the orientation of the role, the most suitable location for staff and the type of person to be employed.

The potential roles for support staff, suggested in previous sections are:

1. building collective affiliation through a tutoring program;

2. assisting students to reorient their conceptions of knowledge and adapt to the conventions of tertiary study;

3. enhancing collective affiliation by assisting students with administrative problems; and

4. counseling students on integrating study demands with work, family and social obligations.

The first issue for discussion is the extent to which these roles can and should be combined. The development of integration is central to the model. Of the facets of integration, collective affiliation is more likely to be developed by sustained contact with an individual than by a succession of short contacts with diverse people. Further, contacts may not happen unless the student is familiar with the member of the institution. Students may be reluctant to initiate contact with a specialist counselor but may feel comfortable discussing a problem with a tutor or local liaison officer with whom they have already had extensive contact.

However, the more the various roles are combined, the more difficult it becomes to find individuals capable of and willing to perform the diverse facets of the combined role. The extent to which roles can be combined depends on the locality of the support staff.

In the discussion of collective affiliation it was suggested that localizing administrative support might maximize collective affiliation. The model might therefore be taken as indicating the desirability of locating support staff wherever students are to be found. However the desirability of such a luxurious provision of student support must be tempered by its cost, particularly when the student population is dispersed.

The cost rises considerably if tutoring support is dispersed, since it becomes necessary to provide expertise in different subject areas. While it may be economical to provide a general administrative support person in a particular location, providing tutors for numerous courses would cost far more, and each tutor might only be relevant for a very small number of students. Providing local tutors only seems to have been considered economically viable for courses with large enrollments (which usually restricts the provision to introductory courses) and where students are reasonably concentrated in particular areas. Otherwise teleconference tutorials have been seen as more efficient, or no group tutoring has been provided. Therefore, of the roles listed at the beginning of this section, there will be only a limited number of courses for which it is possible to provide local tutorial support. This conclusion should not, however, be taken as implying that the provision of local tutorials is discouraged.

Of the remaining listed roles, 3 and 4 can be performed efficiently by staff without expertise in the subject area for which the student has enrolled. It should be possible to find people with the skills necessary for combining these two roles. The employment of local support staff for these two roles is therefore recommended.

The remaining support role is that of assisting students to reorient their conceptions of knowledge and adapt to the conventions of tertiary study as support for other discussed learning skills type initiatives. Human support could be provided for a limited number of workshops, possibly in the style described by Gibbs (1981), in which students reflect upon their approaches to assigned learning tasks.

Gibbs (1981, p. 4) reports having probably moved away from running exercises with groups of students studying mixed courses in favor of students studying the same material. However, he associates advantages and disadvantages with both types of group. It, therefore, seems practicable for a study center officer to act as a convenor for structured discussions for groups of students located close to each other but taking diverse courses. Training for the local support staff would be needed, as few would have experience of running such structured discussion sessions.

There are institutions which employ part-time, and sometimes full-time, staff to provide non subject-specific assistance, though their brief would not necessarily encompass the three roles proposed in this Chapter. Such staff are often associated with a study center, though this is not always the case. Timmins (1986) and Waqa (1984) provide two descriptions of institutions which employ local support staff. Livingston (1985) and Walker (1982) have described centers which offer local support to students enrolled with a number of institutions.

Conclusion

Faculty and colleges often see their involvement with students as limited to strictly academic areas. Persuading faculty to take a wider pastoral interest in the progress of their students and the demands they face can be difficult. It means that faculty have to see their role as rather wider than purely teaching their subject.

While some are resistant to this wider perspective it is interesting how rewarding faculty can find their contact with mature part-time students. As most are well established in relevant careers they bring a perspective and experience to their study which high school graduates do not possess. Many faculty who take a little time to become familiar with their students find that it is not just the students who benefit from the experience.

In addition to wider faculty involvement, the provision of localized support is advocated. This support might encompass advice on enrollment and other administrative procedures. There could be a general counseling role. It would be useful to provide assistance with learning skills through a self-reflection approach. Local tutoring is also desirable, but likely to be more cost-effective through a teleconference medium.

Chapter 16

Conclusions and Future Directions

Synopsis

The model developed in this book could serve as a basis for planning and decision making for institutions which offer open learning and distance education courses. The wide diversity of formats for such courses, even when similar subjects are taught, is an indication that in the past there has been limited guidance from the available literature to decision makers.

The model might also serve as a stimulus for research. There are many propositions within the model worthy of testing. The wide variety of open learning, distance education and adult education courses and the heterogeneity of their setting and environment means that there are numerous contexts in which some or all of the model might be tested. In applying the model in new situations, there is no doubt that it will need to be modified and developed just as this model adapted the ideas of Tinto for application in a quite different setting. Hopefully out of this work will come new and better models.

Approach to Research

Various writers have criticized both the quality and the quantity of research in distance education or open learning (e.g., Childs, 1969; Coldeway, 1982; Ljoså, 1980). While there is a reasonably extensive literature on the subject, much of it has been criticized as being descriptive (Garrison, 1987), or not research at all (Coldeway, 1982). There has also been criticism that practitioners have paid insufficient attention to theory which has been developed (Coldeway, 1987) or of a gap between practice and scholarship (Calvert, 1988). Moore (1985) has also noted that writers of published material often seem unaware of previous research.

Each of these comments by reviewers of research output is symptomatic of a wide tendency towards pragmatism in open learning. The priority has been towards getting courses off the ground rather than developing a theory base to inform better practice.

This position is perfectly understandable, especially when resources are stretched, which is often the case. In the long run, however, it becomes problematic. Unless there is some attempt to devote energy and resources to research and theory building, the practice of open learning will be unable to move beyond intuitive approaches to formulating programs.

A symptom of the limited attention to deriving a theory base is the wide diversity of formats adopted for the same types of course in similar environments. Why, for example, do some courses have compulsory residential schools, while others have no direct contact at all? Why do some courses deliver content through a study package, while others have instructors giving lectures by video channels? Once post-hoc rationale and tradition have been stripped away, the answer to questions like these invariably comes down to the preferences, or even whims, of the program originators. Without an adequate theory base, though, it is not possible to move beyond basing decisions upon individual preferences, however carefully thought through. Once a practice becomes established, it is difficult to change even if subsequently developed theory or more practical evaluation shows the original policy to be flawed.

If distance education research is to provide insights which enable practitioners to base decisions upon sound theory rather than intuition, it also needs to address the issue of generalizability. Hardly any existing research studies have looked beyond a single course or a single institution. It has been very rare for a research design to be replicated in a different situation to see whether similar conclusions could be drawn. Without well defined research paradigms or methodological standards for particular issues, it has not been possible to utilize meta-analysis as has been the case for other educational issues or fields (see e.g., Kulik and Kulik, 1989).

The research reported in this book has attempted to address the issue of generalizability and hence contribute a theory or model which is capable of guiding practice. Firstly, the derivation of the model from qualitative data followed a multi-site approach

(Miles & Huberman, 1984). Inferences were drawn from the work of several researchers in four countries, which are radically different in nature. The model which was developed was then tested twice with independent samples of students from different sets of courses from different institutions. As a result the model generated in the book has every right to claim that the findings should have a high degree of validity and applicability with respect to other open learning programs.

A common feature of the qualitative data used in the projects was that it was derived from semi-structured open-ended interviews or questions. As a result the student perspective is inherent in the model. The research methodology, therefore, answers a criticism by Morgan (1984) that distance education had been over-reliant on a technical rationalist perspective in research. He argued in favor of a wider use of a second-order phenomenological perspective (Marton & Svensson, 1979) which sought insight from the perspective of the student.

The result of this more open initial perspective has been the inclusion within the model of the social integration component. The model recognizes the major impact upon student progress from the work, family and social environments. As students of open learning courses are invariably part-time, these spheres outside the college arena are a major determinant as to the success of the student. Other studies, though, which have started from a more rationalist researcher-centered perspective have ignored this environment altogether and concentrated exclusively on variables within the college system. The result is that these alternative models exclude a vital segment of the explanation of student progress.

Implications

As the model takes a comprehensive approach to explaining student progress it is replete with implications for practice, testable hypotheses and issues which need further researching. Many of these have been drawn out in Part D of the book. In this conclusion it is worth bringing together and re-stating some of the more prominent issues.

Sources of Theory

At the start of this chapter I cited various reviewers' opinions that distance educators had not been prolific researchers, and that much of what had been written was descriptive. The corollary of this position is that there is a limited theory base which is specific to distance education or open learning. If distance education were a discrete discipline it would have an impoverished store of wisdom on which to draw. In reality, though, distance education is a sub-discipline of the wide field of education, with significant overlaps with many other sub-disciplines. There is, then, a voluminous literature from these overlapping educational disciplines on which to draw.

The issue is then to decide which of the spheres of education are most pertinent, and the extent to which findings can be applied to an open learning context. Dealing with the second question first, the consistent message of this book has been that imported models need adaptation if they are to fit the open learning scenario. The most significant characteristics to be fitted are the fact that most of the learning takes place at a distance from the teacher, and students have a part-time status. Unless an imported theory already addresses these two conditions, it needs to be adapted if it is have any credibility.

Educational theories drawn from spheres which most closely pertain to the conditions of open learning will be those which require the least adaptation. For this reason I have drawn upon adult learning theory, to the extent of incorporating the assumptions of andragogy into a revised definition of open learning. I believe that those involved in open learning should recognize that their students are almost invariably adults and thus take note of findings from adult education. Those who wear the label "adult educator" might in turn take greater cognizance of open learning. I suspect that the level of publications on open learning in the adult education literature is well below the proportion of the adult student population enrolled in open learning courses.

If those in open learning do pay greater heed to the adult education literature, they are more likely to recognize the implications of having adult part-time students. They should recognize the major impact upon persistence and performance of the work, family and social environments. To most part-time students, their academic study is an addition to an, often heavy, array of commitments and obligations. Any view of student progress confined to a narrow academic sphere of influence will, then, ignore one of the most fundamental impacts upon the learning outcomes.

Students Internalizing Responsibility

The model proposed in this book does deal with the issue of integrating study demands into the social environment. It suggests that successful students are those who internalize responsibility for their own progress. These students negotiate with their families, work colleagues and friends to establish a time slot for study. The negotiating process is almost inevitably accompanied by mutual sacrifices by both the student and the immediate family. Those unable or unwilling to makes sacrifices and negotiate a study sanctuary tend towards the negative track and to attributing any unsuccessful outcomes to factors external to their control.

The social integration component of the model is ripe for further research and replete with policy implications. A major challenge is to develop programs and short introductory courses which counsel students away from external attributions and towards successful social integration. It is much easier to diagnose these conditions than to develop counseling programs which assist students to take the positive track. If the outcomes of any such programs are properly researched, then there should be a contribution to both theory and practice.

Support for Open Entry Policies

Of the facets of openness in the description of open learning, open access would be seen as the most significant by most people. Open access policies provide an entry to higher education for those who do not meet the traditional entry criteria. A second chance is provided for those who left school early or did not obtain sufficiently good grades for college entrance.

The research cited in this book provides ample support for open access policies for adult students. The qualitative data contains numerous examples of students, many of whom were traditionally unqualified, adapting to the demands of part-time study and learning how to succeed in an academic course. The quantitative data shows that the efforts of the students and the quality of the instruction and support provided by the college have a greater impact upon student progress than the qualifications at entry.

The model reflects this finding by incorporating a recycling loop. Students can switch tracks either by their own commitment and determination or because of the impact of the support and instruction. There is, therefore, a clear incentive for the college to optimize the quality of its services to maximize the chance of student progress.

Measuring Persistence

Some level of attrition is inevitable, however well the institution fine-tunes its instruction and services. Colleges should, though, look at their data on student outcomes. It may never be possible for every enrolled student to graduate, but improvement should be possible. Student progress statistics can be used as an indicator of the effectiveness of improvement measures. The ideal would be for colleges to move towards a climate of continual monitoring and searching for improvement akin to a total quality management approach.

For student progress statistics to be of value, there does need to be a distinction made between the various paths by which students can complete or not complete a course of study. Figure 2-1 shows the way data could be portrayed if they are to provide the information necessary for valid decision making. Some institutions might have to adapt their recording procedures to make available data for all the paths.

Instruction

Deep approach and intrinsic motivation appeared in the positive track of the model, so instructional design should concentrate upon encouraging meaningful learning and developing interest in courses. As traditional instructional design models have not always addressed these issues, there is a need for the development of new models which take account of the research into student learning. There is also, of course, a need to research and test the effectiveness of courses based upon these newer models.

There are suggestions in Chapter 13 as to the way instructional design might develop. A focus on quality rather than quantity is advocated. It is more important for students to thoroughly understand the key concepts of a subject than to attempt to memorize factual information. This implies top-down sequencing strategies rather than the bricks-building wall approach.

Student Support

The model also advances testable hypotheses for the format of student support services. The aim of these services should be to enhance collective affiliation and normative congruence. The implication I draw in Chapters 14 and 15 is that this could perhaps best be achieved by a policy of localizing support services to a study center network or to local liaison officers. Teleconference facilities would be more usefully employed for promoting interaction with and between students, than for transmitting course content. I also believe that there should be a greater exploration of the use of group work.

Further Development and Testing of the Model

Models are inevitably simplified versions of reality. They can only aim to select the more important variables in a complex problem, so as to provide a manageable insight into the issues. In quantitative terms this model, like other similar ones, explains only a proportion of the variance.

If this model helps readers to better visualize the determinants of progress for part-time student in open learning courses, it will have some value. Models, though, should not be seen as immutable. They are of greatest value if they are tested, adapted, developed and improved. Open learning courses are now so widespread and diverse in nature that there are many contexts and cultures, quite different from those examined in this book, in which the model might be tested. Just as this model grew out of a need to adapt another model, I have no doubt that my model in turn will need adaptation if it is to suit some of the more divergent forms of open learning. Hopefully the process of testing and adoption of the model will lead to new insights which can eventually be incorporated into new and better models.

Figure 16-1: The full model of student progress

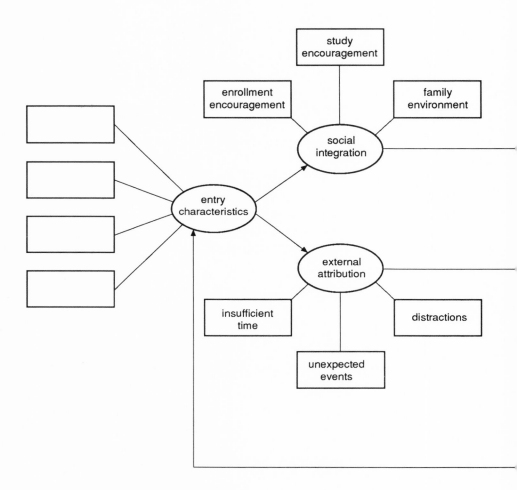

Figure 16-1: continued

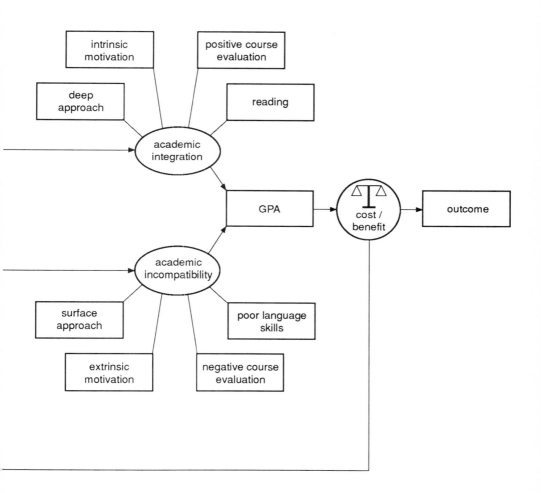

Summary

To provide a summary and conclusion to this chapter and to the book, I revert to the model in its graphic form. The rationale for the book was the lack of suitable tested models for open learning. The book has been about developing and testing a model and then drawing implications from it. It, therefore seems fitting to end with a display of the model as a whole.

The preceding two page spread shows the full model. Each of the major components are shown in ovals. They have their full array of sub-components, shown in rectangles, branching from them. GPA and the final outcome measure are also shown in rectangles. The model also includes the cost/benefit balance and a recycling loop.

Appendix A

Interview Schedule

Introduction

The following two items are © David Kember, Tammy Lai, David Murphy, Irene Siaw and K.S. Yuen, except for questions adapted from the Approaches to Studying Inventory.

Interview Schedule
in Appendix A

Distance Education Student Progress Inventory
in Appendix B

We are happy for other researchers to make use of either the DESP inventory or the interview schedule for research or professional use, which does not result in commercial gain to the user. We ask that appropriate acknowledgments and references are made in any resulting publications. Use of the inventory or interview schedule is on the understanding that copyright remains with its original authors.

Both the inventory and interview schedule are likely to need some adaptation for use in other situations. The interview schedule might be treated more as a guide to potential questions than as a script to be followed closely.

Interview Schedule

The interview schedule is designed to be used very loosely—more as suggestions for topics for a conversation than as a set of questions to be followed word for word. The aim of a semi-structured interview should be to allow the student to talk freely on topics within the area of interest. The introductory comments, questions and probes used in the interviews are listed below. Possible prompts are shown in italics.

Introductory Comments

This interview is part of an evaluation project which aims to find out how to help distance learning students to succeed in their courses. To achieve this aim we need to find out how effective the study materials and student support is. We also need to ask how your work, family and social commitment affect your studies. By giving this information it will help us plan better courses for you and your fellow students.

This interview should last about 30 minutes. We would like to tape record it so that we have an accurate record of what you say. The interview tapes will only be available to the research workers in this project.

You will not be identified by name in any report we write. If short extracts are quoted from interviews, students will not be identified personally.

Are you happy to take part in the interview on this basis?

Education

How long ago did you leave school?
After which grade did you leave school?
Have you taken any courses since learning school?
Why did you enroll in this course?
What do you like most and what do you like least about being a distance learning student?
If it were possible which mode of study would you prefer?
Full-time
Part-time classes
Distance learning
Why?
Do you find the course interesting?
Enjoy reading matter
Content

Presentation
Design
Is the material in the course relevant to your job?

Study Materials and Study Method

When you read the study materials do you follow the order in which it is presented?
If not—what order?
Do you do the questions and activities suggested in the study booklets?
Why?
Why not?
Do you do them all?
Do you write down answers or think about the questions?
Do you set aside a specific time slot each week for studying?
Is there any study technique or method you adopt when reading the course materials or textbooks?
How many times do you read the material?
Do you write notes ?
What do you think of the study materials?

Tutorial Support

Did you attend the tutorials?
If not—why not?
If you did—did you find them helpful? Why?
Did you use the telephone counseling service?
If not—why not?
If you did—did you find it helpful?
What did you ask about?
Did you have study or personal problems but felt that the tutors would not be able to help you with them?
Would you tell me about them?
Were the comments on returned assignments helpful?
Do you think you need help/communication with a tutor/lecturer or are the study materials enough?
Which methods of communication do you like:
Face-to-face class
Face-to-face, one-to-one

Telephone counseling

Do you feel that your lecturers/tutors are remote and distant or are they people who are friendly and easy to deal with?

Do you feel as though you belong to your college/university even though you are a distance learning student?

Could you expand on that a little?

Do you use any of the university facilities?

Do you talk to other students?

If so how often?

and about what?

Administration

Was the course administered well?

Study material delivery

Assignment return prompt

Instructions clear

Staff helpful

Could any aspect of the administration be improved?

Home/Work/Social

Where do you study?

Is it a good place for study?

What work do you do?

Position

Type of work

Hours (regular/overtime)

Travel

How does your work affect your study?

Has taking the course helped with your work?

Do you have a family?

Do they affect your study?

How does your study affect them?

Do your friends affect your study?

Has your social life changed since you started the course?

Expectations and Impressions

Before starting the course, how confident did you feel about your ability to succeed as a distance learning student?
Is the course what you expected?
Was the work for the course very different to what you expected?
Do you ever feel discouraged from doing the course?
Do you ever come close to giving it up?
What goes through your mind?
Assuming you complete the course, how will you benefit from the qualification?
Overall, has it been worthwhile enrolling in this course as a distance learning student?

Appendix B

Distance Education Student Progress Inventory

The initial demographic questions in the DESP instrument may need to be altered for use outside Hong Kong, though demographic items thought to be peculiar to Hong Kong have not been included here. The wording of some items in the instrument may have to be modified to suit local terminology or student support facilities featured in a course. The inventory is presented as a list of items under headings showing the scales and sub-scales they contribute to. These headings did not appear in the questionnaire given to students. In the questionnaire all items were numbered and appeared in semi-random order.

It should be noted that the following four sub-scales in the inventory have been adapted from the Approaches to Studying Inventory (ASI) (Entwistle and Ramsden, 1983):

- deep approach,
- intrinsic motivation,
- surface approach, and
- extrinsic motivation.

Apart from the background characteristics questions, students were asked to respond to items using a five point Likert scale (Definitely agree/Agree with reservations/Only to be used if the item does not apply to you or if you find it impossible to give a definite answer/Disagree with reservations/Definitely disagree).

Four items indicated with a star (*) have to be reverse scored as they were written in the opposite sense to other items in the sub-scale .

Background Characteristics

Age :_____ years old
How many children do you have?_____
How many years of working experience do you have?_____
How many people live together in your home? _____
Course (courses listed)
Sex (Male/Female)
Marital status (Married/Single)
How long do you take to travel from your place of residence to the college/university? (4 categories)
What is your present monthly salary? (8 categories)
Please indicate the type of secondary school you attended. (5 categories)
What is your highest qualification? (6 categories)

Social Integration

Enrollment Encouragement (4 items)

My spouse encouraged me to enroll in this course.
My family encouraged me to enroll in this course.
My employer encouraged me to enroll in this course.
My friends encouraged me to enroll in this course.

Study Encouragement (4 items)

My employer was supportive while I was studying.
My spouse offered support while I was studying.
My workmates encouraged me to study.
My family encouraged me to study because they thought the qualification was important.

Family Support (3 items)

I usually spend a lot of time with my family.
* I don't need the support of my family to succeed in this course.
The support of my family means a lot to me.

External Attribution

Insufficient Time *(4 items)*

As I work long hours it is difficult to find time to study.
Long hours at work left little time for study.
I seem to have so many other things to do there is never enough time for study.
A change in my work left me without enough time for study.

Events Hinder Study *(3 items)*

A change to my work situation made it difficult to complete the course.
I was ill during the course, so found it difficult to keep up.
Personal/family circumstances, unseen at the time of enrollment, hindered my studies.

Distractions *(7 items)*

I prefer to spend time doing things other than studying.
I have a busy social life.
I went out a lot, rather than studying.
My spouse became annoyed because I spent so much time studying.
My children interfered with my studies.
* I do not let anything interfere with my studies.
My friends wanted me to go out rather than study.

Potential Drop-out *(3 items)*

* I am very determined to finish the course.
I often consider dropping out from the course.
I often wonder whether all the study is worth the effort.

Academic Integration

Deep Approach (4 items)

I generally put a lot of effort into trying to understand things which seem difficult at first.
I usually set out to understand thoroughly the meaning of what I am asked to read.
When I'm tackling a new topic, I often ask myself questions about it which the new information should answer.
I often find myself questioning things that I read in books or study materials.

Intrinsic Motivation (4 items)

My main reason for doing this course is so that I can learn more about the subjects which really interest me.
I find that studying academic topics can often be really exciting.
I spend a good deal of my spare time in finding out more about interesting topics in the course.
I find academic topics so interesting, I should like to continue with them after I finish this course.

Positive Course Evaluation (5 items)

I found the study guide useful in preparing for the course.
The activities/self-assessment questions have helped me to learn.
The study booklets are easy to learn from.
The tutor's comments on my assignments have helped me to study.
The course was administered very efficiently.

Positive Telephone Counseling (4 items)

The telephone counseling service is useful.
The telephone counseling service provided help when I needed it.
* Telephone counseling is a waste of time.
I use the telephone counseling service often.

Reading Habit (3 *items*)

I enjoy reading so I am suited to distance learning courses.
I read other books as well as the study materials and set texts.
I read widely.

Academic Incompatibility

Surface Approach (6 *items*)

Lecturers seem to delight in making the simple truth unnecessarily complicated.
The best way for me to understand what technical terms mean is to remember the text-book definitions.
I find I have to concentrate on memorizing a good deal of what I have to learn.
When I'm reading I try to memorize important facts which may come in useful later.
I usually don't have time to think about the implications of what I have read.
Often I find I have read things without having a chance to really understand them.

Extrinsic Motivation (4 *items*)

I suppose I am more interested in the qualifications I'll get than in the course I'm taking.
I chose the present course mainly to give me a chance of a really good job afterwards.
I generally choose what I study more from the way it fits in with career plans than from my own interests.
My main reason doing this course is that it will help me to get a better job.

Negative Course Evaluation (6 *items*)

The learning materials are presented in a confusing way.
I do not understand a lot of English words in the study materials.
The type of work required by assignments is very different from what I expected.

The course is not run at the most suitable time of the year.
The assignments are too difficult.
The time allowed for completing the course is too short.

English Ability (4 items)

What grade were you awarded in English Language in the (appropriate) examination? (9 categories)
Please grade your English ability:
Writing (Excellent/Very good/Good/Poor/Very Poor)
Reading (Excellent/Very good/Good/Poor/Very Poor)
Speaking (Excellent/Very good/Good/Poor/Very Poor)

References

Abel, W.H. (1966). Attrition and the student who is certain. *Personnel and Guidance Journal, 44*, 1942-1045.

Argyris, C. & Schön, D. (1978). *Organizational learning: A theory-of-action perspective.* Reading, MA: Addison-Wesley.

Ausubel, D.P. (1960). The use of advance organizers in the learning and retention of meaningful verbal material. *Journal of Educational Psychology, 63*, 267-272.

Ausubel, D.P. (1968). *Educational psychology. A cognitive view.* New York: Holt, Rinehart and Winston.

Ausubel, D.P. (1978). In defense of advance organizers: A reply to the critics. *Review of Educational Research, 48*, 251-257.

Bååth, J.A. (1980). *Postal two-way communication in correspondence education.* Malmo: Liber Hermods.

Bååth, J.A. (1984). Research on completion and discontinuation in distance education. *Epistolodidaktika, 1*, 31-43.

Baird, J.R. & White, R.T. (1982). Promoting self-control of learning. *Instructional Science, 11*, 227-247.

Bar-Tal, D. (1978). Attributional analysis of achievement-related behavior. *Review of Educational Research, 48*, 259-271.

Barnes, B.R. & Clawson, E.U. (1975). Do advance organizers facilitate learning? Recommendations for further research based on an analysis of 32 studies. *Review of Educational Research, 45*, 637-659.

Barron. R.F. (1969). The use of vocabulary as an advance organizer. In H.L. Herber & P.L. Sanders (Eds.), *Research in reading in the content areas: First year report.* Syracuse University: Reading and Language Arts Center.

Bean, J.P. (1979). *Path analysis: The development of a suitable methodology for the study of student attrition.* Paper presented at the annual meeting of the American Educational Research Association, San Francisco, California, April 1979.

Bean, J.P. (1982). Conceptual models of student attrition: How theory can help the institutional researcher. In E.T. Pascarella (Ed.), *Studying student attrition.* San-Francisco: Jossey-Bass.

Bean, J.P. (1983). The application of a model of turnover in work organizations to the student attrition process. *Review of Higher Education, 6*, 129-148.

Bean, J.P. & Metzner, B.S. (1985). A conceptual model of non-traditional undergraduate student attrition. *Review of Educational Research, 55*, 485-540.

Bernard, R.M. & Amundsen, C.L. (1989). Antecedents to dropout in distance education: Does one model fit all? *Journal of Distance Education, 4*(2), 25-46.

Biggs, J. (1987). *Student approaches to learning and studying.* Melbourne: Australian Council for Educational Research.

Biggs, J.B. (Ed.) (1991). *Teaching for learning: The view from cognitive psychology.* Melbourne: Australian Council for Educational Research.

Billings, D.M. (1988). A conceptual model of correspondence course completion. *American Journal of Distance Education, 2*(2), 23-35.

Blanchfield, W.C. (1971). College dropout identification: A case study. *Journal of Experimental Education, 40*, 1-4.

Bonner, J. (1988). Implications of cognitive theory for instructional design: Revisited. *Educational Communications and Technology Journal, 36*(1), 3-14.

Boshier, R. (1971). Motivational orientations of adult education participants: A factor analytic exploration of Houle's typology. *Adult Education Journal, 21*(2), 3-26.

Boshier, R. (1972). The development and use of a dropout prediction scale. *Adult Education, 22*(2), 87-99.

Boshier, R. (1973). Educational participation and dropout: A theoretical model. *Adult Education, 23*(4), 255-282.

Bowden, J. (1988). Achieving change in teaching practices. In P. Ramsden (Ed.), *Improving learning: New perspectives.* London: Kogan Page.

Bowden, J.A. (1989). *Curriculum development for conceptual change learning: A phenomenographic pedagogy.* Paper presented to the sixth annual conference of the Hong Kong Educational Research Association, Hong Kong.

Bowser, D. & Race, K. (1991). Orientation for distance education students: What is its worth? *Distance Education, 12*(1), 109-122.

Brindley, J.E. (1988). A model of attrition for distance education. In D. Sewart & J.S. Daniel (Eds.), *Developing distance education.* Oslo: International Council for Distance Education.

Brody, P.J. (1982). Affecting instructional textbooks through pictures. In D.H. Jonassen (Ed.), *The technology of text: Principles for structuring, designing and displaying text.* Englewood Cliffs, NJ: Educational Technology Publications.

Brookfield, S.D. (1986). *Understanding and facilitating adult learning.* Milton Keynes: Open University Press.

Brower, A.M. (1992). The 'second half' of student integration. *Journal of Higher Education, 63*(4), 441-462.

Cabrera, A.F., Castañeda, M.B., Nora, A. & Hengstler, D. (1992). The convergence between two theories of college persistence. *Journal of Higher Education , 63*(2), 143-164.

Calvert, J. (1988). Distance education research: The rocky courtship of scholarship and practice. *ICDE Bulletin.*

Centre for Educational Research and Innovation (1987). *Adults in higher education.* Paris: Centre for Economic Co-operation and Development.

Chacon, F.J. (1985). A multivariate model for evaluating distance higher education. Unpublished doctoral thesis, Pennsylvania State University.

Champagne, A.B., Gunstone, R.F. & Klopfer, L.E. (1985). Effecting changes in cognitive structures among physics students. In L.H.T. West & A.L. Pines (Eds.), *Cognitive structure and conceptual change.* New York: Academic Press.

Champagne, A.B., Klopfer, L.E., DeSena, A.T. & Squires, D.A. (1981). Structural representations of students' knowledge before and after science instruction. *Journal of Research in Science Teaching, 18,* 91-111.

Chase, C.I. (1970). The college dropout: His high school prologue. *Bulletin of the National Association of Secondary School Principals, 54,* 66-71.

Childs, G.B. (1969). Report of the chairman of the committee on research. *Proceedings of the 8th International Conference, International Council for Correspondence Education.* Paris.

Christie, N.G. & Dinham, S.M. (1991). Institutional and external influences on social integration in the freshman year. *Journal of Higher Education , 62*(4), 412-436.

Clyde, A., Crowther, M., Patching, W., Putt, I. & Store, R. (1983). How students use distance teaching materials: An institutional case study. *Distance Education, 4*(1), 4-26.

Coldeway, D.O. (1982). Recent research in distance learning. In J.S. Daniel, M.A. Stroud & J.R. Thompson (Eds.), *Learning at a distance: A world perspective*. Edmonton: Athabasca University/ICDE.

Coldeway, D.O. (1987). Behavior analysis in distance education: A systems perspective. *American Journal of Distance Education, 1*, 7-20.

Connors, B. (1980) Assessment of students in distance teaching. In J.D. Armstrong & R.E. Store (Eds.), *Evaluation in distance teaching*. Townsville, Queensland: Townsville College of Advanced Education.

Cookson, P.S. (1990). Persistence in distance education: A review. In M.G. Moore (Ed.), *Contemporary issues in American distance education*. Oxford: Pergamon Press.

Cope, R. & Hannah, W. (1975). *Revolving college doors*. New York: John Wiley and Sons.

Dahlgren, L.O. (1978). *Qualitative differences in conceptions of basic principles in economics*. Paper read to the 4th International Conference on Higher Education at Lancaster, August/ September 1978.

Dahlgren, L.O. (1984). Outcomes of learning. In F. Marton, D. Hounsell & N. Entwistle (Eds.), *The experience of learning*. Edinburgh: Scottish Academic Press.

Dahlgren, L.O. & Marton, F. (1978). Students' conceptions of subject matter: An aspect of learning and teaching in higher education. *Studies in Higher Education, 3*, 25-35.

Dart, B.C. & Clarke, J.A. (1991). Helping students become better learners: A case study in teacher education. *Higher Education, 23*, 317-335.

Davies, H., Sivan, A. & Kember, D. (in press). Helping Hong Kong Business students to appreciate how they learn. *Higher Education*.

Day, C. & Baskett, H.K. (1982). Discrepancies between intentions and practice: Reexamining some basic assumptions about adult and continuing professional education. *International Journal of Lifelong Education, 1*(2), 143-155.

Deci, E. L. (1975). *Intrinsic motivation*. New York: Plenum Press.

Dewey, J. (1929). *The sources of a science of education*. New York: Horace Liveright.

Dille, B. & Mezack, M. (1991). Identifying predictors of high risk among community college telecourse students. *American Journal of Distance Education, 5*(1), 24-35.

Driver, R. & Erickson, G. (1983). Theories-in-action: Some theoretical and empirical issues in the study of students' conceptual frameworks. *Studies in Science Education, 10*, 37-60.

Driver, R. & Oldham, V. (1985). A constructivist approach to curriculum in science. Paper prepared for the Symposium *Personal Construction of Meaning in Educational Settings*, British Educational Research Association, Sheffield, August.

Duncan, O.D. (1966). Path analysis: Sociological examples. *The American Journal of Sociology, 72*, 1-16.

Durkheim, E. (1961). *Suicide* (Spaulding, J. & Simpson, G. Trans.). Glencoe: The Free Press.

Eizenberg, N. (1986). Applying student learning research to practice. In J.A. Bowden (Ed.), *Student learning: Research into practice*. Melbourne: The University of Melbourne.

Entwistle, N.J. & Ramsden, P. (1983). *Understanding student learning*. London: Croom Helm.

Fay, P. (1988). Open and student centred learning: Evangelism and heresy. *Journal of Further and Higher Education, 12*(1), 3-19.

Finkel, A. (1985). Teaching history at a distance. *Distance Education, 6*, 1, 56-67.

Fishbein, M. & Ajzen, I. (1975). *Belief, attitude, intention and behavior: An introduction to theory and research*. Reading, MA: Addison-Wesley.

Fleming, A. (1982) The Allama Iqbal Open University. In G. Rumble & K. Harry (Eds.), *The distance teaching universities*. London: Croom Helm.

Fleming, M. & Levie, W.H. (Eds.) (1993). *Instructional message design: Principles from the behavioral and cognitive sciences* (2nd. edition). Englewood Cliffs, NJ: Educational Technology Publications.

Flinck, R. (1978). *Correspondence education combined with systematic telephone tutoring*. Malmo: Liber Hermods.

Ford, N. (1981). Recent approaches to the study and teaching of effective learning in higher education. *Review of Educational Research, 51*(3), 345-377.

Fransson, A. (1977) On qualitative differences in learning. IV-Effects of motivation and test anxiety on process and outcome. *British Journal of Educational Psychology, 47*, 244-257.

Gagné, R.M. (1968). Learning hierarchies. *Educational Psychologist, 6*, 3-6.

Garrison, D.R. (1987) Researching dropout in distance education. *Distance Education, 8*(1), 95-101.

Garrison, D.R. (1993). A cognitive constructivist view of distance education: An analysis of teaching-learning assumptions. *Distance Education, 14*(2), 199-211.

Gibbs, G. (1981). *Teaching students to learn: A student-centred approach*. Milton Keynes: Open University Press.

Gibbs, G. (1984). Better teaching or better learning. *HERDSA News, 6*, 1.

Glaser, B.G. & Strauss, A.L. (1967). *The discovery of grounded theory*. Chicago: Aldine.

Glatter, R. & Wedell, E.G. (1971). *Study by correspondence*. London: Longman.

Goldschmid, B. & Goldschmid, M.L. (1976). Peer teaching in higher education: A review. *Higher Education, 5*, 9-33.

Goodlad, S. & Hirst, B. (1989). *Peer tutoring: A guide to learning by teaching*. London: Kogan Page.

Gow, L. & Kember, D. (1990). Does higher education promote independent learning? *Higher Education, 19*, 307-322.

Gow, L. & Kember, D. (1993). Conceptions of teaching and their relationship to student learning. *British Journal of Educational Psychology, 63*, 20-33.

Gow, L., Kember, D. & Chow, R. (1991). The effects of English language ability on approaches to learning. *RELC Journal, 22*(1), 49-68.

Gunstone, R.F. & White, R.T. (1981). Understanding of gravity. *Science Education, 65*, 291-299.

Halldén, O. (1986). Learning history. *Oxford Review of Education, 12*, 53-66.

Hartree, A. (1984). Malcolm Knowles theory of andragogy: A critique. *International Journal of Lifelong Education, 3*(3), 203-210.

Hawk, P., McLeod, N.P. & Jonassen, D.H. (1985). Graphic organizers in texts, courseware, and supplemental material. In D.H. Jonassen (Ed.), *The technology of text: Principles for structuring, designing, and displaying text (Vol. 2)*. Englewood Cliffs, NJ: Educational Technology Publications.

Helm, H. & Novak, J.D. (1983). *Misconceptions in science and mathematics*. Ithaca, NY: Cornell University.

Holmberg, B. (1985). *Status and trends of distance education*. Lund: Lector.

Hounsell, D.J. (1984). Learning and essay-writing. In F. Marton, D. Hounsell & N. Entwistle (Eds.), *The experience of learning*. Edinburgh: Scottish Academic Press.

Howard, D.C. (1985). Reading and study skills and the distance learner. *Distance Education, 6*(2), 169-188.

Idle, G. (1980). Mature-age non-starters. *ASPESA Newsletter, 6*(2), 9-13.

Jaffe, A. & Adams, W. (1970). Academic and socio-economic factors related to entrance and retention at two- and four-year colleges in the late 1960's. *Proceedings of the American Statistical Association*, Social Statistics Section.

Jaques, D. (1984). *Learning in groups*. London: Croom Helm.

Jonassen, D.H. (1985). Generative learning vs. mathemagenic control of text processing. In D.H. Jonassen (Ed.), *The technology of text: Principles for structuring, designing, and displaying text (Vol. 2)*. Englewood Cliffs, NJ: Educational Technology Publications.

Kearney, J.E. (1969). Success factors in a tertiary institution. *Australian Journal of Higher Education, 3*(3), 231-237.

Keegan, D.J. (1986). *The foundations of distance education*. London: Croom Helm.

Keller, J.M. (1983). Motivational design of instruction. In C.M. Reigeluth (Ed.), *Instructional-design theories and models: An overview of their current status*. Hillsdale, NJ: Lawrence Erlbaum Associates.

Keller, J.M. (1987). Development and use of the ARCS model of instructional design. *Journal of Instructional Development, 10*(3), 2-10.

Kember, D. (1981). Some factors affecting attrition and performance in a distance education course at the University of Papua New Guinea. *Distance Education, 2*(2), 164-188.

Kember, D. (1982). Mature entry for external university courses. *Papua New Guinea Journal of Education, 18*(1), 79-87.

Kember, D. (1985). The use of inserted questions in study material for distance education courses. *ASPESA Newsletter, 11*(1), 12-19.

Kember, D. (1989a) A linear process model of drop-out from distance education. *Journal of Higher Education, 60*(3), 278-301.

Kember, D. (1989b). An illustration, with case-studies, of a linear process model of drop-out from distance education. *Distance Education, 10*(2), 196-211

Kember, D. (1991). Instructional design for meaningful learning. *Instructional Science, 20*, 289-310.

Kember, D. & Dekkers, J. (1987). The role of study centres for academic support in distance education. *Distance Education, 8*(1), 4-17.

Kember, D. & Gow, L. (1989). A model of student approaches to learning encompassing ways to influence and change approaches. *Instructional Science, 18,* 263-288.

Kember, D. & Gow, L. (1994). Orientations to teaching and their effect on the quality of student learning. *Journal of Higher Education.*

Kember, D. & Harper, G. (1987). Implications for instruction arising from the relationship between approaches to studying and academic outcomes. *Instructional Science, 16,* 35-46.

Kember, D., Lai, T., Murphy, D., Siaw, I., Wong, W.Y. & Yuen, K.S. (1990). Naturalistic evaluation of distance learning courses. *Journal of Distance Education, 4*(2), 38-52.

Kember, D., Lai, T., Murphy, D., Siaw, I. & Yuen, K.S. (1992a). Student progress in distance education: Identification of explanatory constructs. *British Journal of Educational Psychology, 62,* 285-298.

Kember, D., Lai, T., Murphy, D., Siaw, I. & Yuen, K.S. (1992b). Demographic characteristics of Hong Kong distance learning students. *ICDE Bulletin, 29,* 24-34.

Kember, D., Lai, T., Murphy, D., Siaw, I. & Yuen, K.S. (1992c). A synthesis of evaluations of distance education courses. *British Journal of Educational Technology, 23*(2), 122-135.

Kember, D. & Murphy, D. (1990). A synthesis of open, distance and student-centred learning. *Open Learning, 5*(2), 3-8.

Kember, D. & Murphy, D. (1994). *53 interesting activities for open learning courses.* Bristol: Technical and Educational Services.

Kember, D., Murphy, D., Siaw, I. & Yuen, K.S. (1991). Towards a causal model of student progress in distance education. *American Journal of Distance Education, 5*(2), 3-15.

Kennedy, D. & Powell, R. (1976). Student progress and withdrawal in the Open University. *Teaching at a Distance, 7,* 61-75.

Kerlinger, F.L. & Pedhazur, E.J. (1973). *Multiple regression in behavioral research.* New York: Holt, Rinehart and Winston.

Kim, J. & Kohout, F. (1975). Multiple regression analysis: Subprogram regression. In N.H. Nie, *et al.* (Eds.),*Statistical package for the social sciences.* New York: McGraw-Hill.

Kirkup, G. (1984). Teaching study skills in context. In E.S. Henderson & M.B. Nathenson (Eds.), *Independent learning in higher education*. Englewood Cliffs, NJ: Educational Technology Publications.

Knoell, D.M. (1966). A critical review of research on the college dropout. In L.A. Pervin, L.E. Reik & W. Dalrymple (Eds.), *The college dropout and the utilization of talent*. Princeton: Princeton University Press.

Knowles, M. (1970). *Modern practice of adult education: Andragogy vs pedagogy*. New York: Association Press.

Knowles, M. (1983). Andragogy: An emerging technology for adult learning. In M. Tight (Ed.), *Adult learning and education*. London: Croom Helm.

Knowles, M. (1984). *The adult learner–a neglected species*. Houston: Gulf Publishing Company.

Knowles, M.S. (1990). *The adult learner: A neglected species* (4th edition). Houston: Gulf.

Kulik, J.A. & Kulik, C.L.C. (1989). Meta analysis in education. *International Journal of Educational Research, 13*(3), 221-340.

Land, K.C. (1969). Principles of path analysis. In E.F. Borgatta (Ed.), *Sociological methodology*. San Francisco: Jossey-Bass.

Laurillard, D. (1984). Learning from problem solving. In F. Marton, D. Hounsell & N. Entwistle (Eds.), *The experience of learning*. Edinburgh: Scottish Academic Press.

Lavin, D. (1965). *The prediction of academic performance*. New York: Russell Sage Foundation.

Lawton, J.T. & Wanska, S.K. (1977). Advance organizers as a teaching strategy: A reply to Barnes and Clawson. *Review of Educational Research, 47*, 233-244.

Lee, S. (1993, September 8). Schooling abroad set for control. *South China Morning Post*, 4.

Lewin, K. (1952). Group decision and social change. In G.E. Swanson, T.M. Newcomb & F.E. Hartley (Eds.), *Readings in social psychology*. New York: Holt.

Lewis, L.H. (1988). *Addressing the needs of returning women*. San Francisco: Jossey-Bass.

Lewis, R. & Spencer, D. (1986). *What is open learning?* London: Council for Educational Technology.

Livingston, K.T. (1985). The education brokering role of the Northern Territory External Studies Centre. In A.S. Castro, K.T. Livingston & P.H. Northcott (Eds.), *An Australian casebook of study centres in distance education*. Geelong: Deakin University, Distance Education Unit.

Ljoså, E. (1980). Some thoughts on the state of research in distance education. *Distance Education, 1*(1), 99-102.

Lochhead, J. (1985). New horizons in educational development. In E.W. Gordon (Ed.), *Review of Research in Education 12*. Washington, DC: AERA.

Luiten, J., Ames, W. & Ackerson, G. (1980). A meta-analysis of the effects of advance organizers on learning and retention. *American Educational Research Journal, 17*, 211-218.

Lybeck, L., Marton, F., Strömdahl, M. & Tullberg, A. (1988). The phenomenography of the 'mole concept' in chemistry. In P. Ramsden (Ed.), *Improving learning: New perspectives*. London: Kogan Page.

Mahony, M.J. & Morgan, C.K. (1991). *A sense of belonging: The unacknowledged dimension of quality in distance education*. Paper presented to the ASPESA biennial forum, Bathurst, NSW, 15-19 July.

Malley, J.I., Brown, A.P. & Williams, J.W. (1976). Drop-outs from external studies: A case study of the investigation process. *Epistolodidaktika, 2*, 170-179.

Manwaring, G. (1986). *Flexibilities: A simulation on the resource implications of open learning*. Scottish Council for Educational Technology.

Marshall, L.A. (1984). *Developing audio learning skills materials for external students*. Paper presented at the Australasian 5th annual study skills conference. Geelong, Victoria.

Martin, E. & Ramsden, P. (1987). Learning skills, or skill in learning. In J.T.E. Richardson, M.W. Eysenck & D.W. Piper (Eds.), *Student learning: Research in education and cognitive psychology*. SRHE and Open University: Milton Keynes.

Marton, F. (1989). *The nature and development of competence*. Paper presented to the sixth annual conference of the Hong Kong Educational Research Association, Hong Kong.

Marton, F., Dall'Alba, G. & Beaty, E. (1993). Conceptions of learning. *International Journal of Educational Research, 19*(3), 277-300.

Marton, F., Hounsell, D. & Entwistle, N. (1984). *The experience of learning*. Edinburgh: Scottish Academic Press.

Marton, F. & Säljö, R. (1976a). On qualitative differences in learning, outcome and process I. *British Journal of Educational Psychology, 46,* 4-11.

Marton, F. & Säljö, R. (1976b). On qualitative differences in learning, outcome and process II. *British Journal of Educational Psychology, 46,* 115-127.

Marton, F. & Svensson, L. (1979). Conceptions of research in student learning. *Higher Education, 8*(4), 471-486.

Marton, F. & Wenestam, C-G. (1978). Qualitative differences in the understanding and retention of the main point in some texts based on the principle-example structure. In M.M. Gruneberg, P.E. Morris & R.N. Sykes (Eds.), *Practical aspects of memory.* London: Academic Press.

Mayer, R.E. (1979). Can advance organizers influence meaningful learning? *Review of Educational Research, 49*(2), 371-383.

McDermott, L.C. (1984). Research on conceptual understanding in mechanics. *Physics Today, 37,* July, 24-32.

McIntosh, Woodley, A. & Morrison, V. (1980). Student demand and progress at the Open University–the first eight years. *Distance Education 1*(1), 37-60.

McKenzie, L. (1977). The issue of andragogy. *Adult Education, 27*(4), 225-229.

Melton, R. (1984). Alternative forms of preliminary organizer: Overview. In E. Henderson & M. Nathenson (Eds.), *Independent learning in higher education.* Englewood Cliffs, NJ: Educational Technology Publications.

Merrill, M.D., Li, Z. & Jones, M.K. (1990). Limitations of first generation instructional design. *Educational Technology, 30* (1), 7-11.

Misanchuk, E.R. (1992). *Preparing instructional text: Document design using desktop publishing.* Englewood Cliffs, NJ: Educational Technology Publications.

Miles, M.B. & Huberman, A. M. (1984). *Qualitative data analysis: A sourcebook of new methods.* Newbury Park, CA: Sage.

Moore, D.W. & Readence, J.E. (1984). A quantitative and qualitative review of graphic organizer research. *Journal of Educational Research, 78,* 11-17.

Moore, M.G. (1985). Some observations on current research in distance education. *Epistolodidaktika, 1,* 35-62.

Morgan, A.A. (1984). A report on qualitative methodologies in research in distance education. *Distance Education, 5*(2), 252-267.

Morris, A. & Stewart-Dore, N. (1984). *Learning to learn from text: Effective reading in the content areas.* North Ryde, NSW: Addison-Wesley.

Munro, B.H. (1981). Dropouts from higher education: Path analysis of a national sample. *American Educational Research Journal, 18* (2), 133-141.

Nation, D. (1987). Some reflections upon teaching Sociology at a distance. *Distance Education, 8*(2), 190-207.

Newble, D. & Clarke, R. (1987). Approaches to learning in a traditional and an innovative medical school. In J.T.E. Richardson, M.W. Eysenk & D.W. Piper (Eds.), *Student learning: Research in education and cognitive psychology.* Milton Keynes: SRHE and Open University.

Northedge, A. (1975). Learning through discussion in the Open University. *Teaching at a Distance, 2,* 10-19.

Novak, J.D. & Gowin, D.B. (1984). *Learning how to learn.* Cambridge: Cambridge University Press.

Nussbaum, J. & Novick, S. (1982). Alternative frameworks, conceptual conflict and accommodation: Toward a principled teaching strategy. *Instructional Science, 11,* 183-200.

Osborne, J., Kilpatrick, S. & Kember, D. (1987). *Student withdrawal survey 1983-86.* Tasmanian State Institute of Technology, mimeograph.

Osborne, R.J. & Wittrock, M.C. (1983). Learning science: A generative process. *Science Education, 67*(4), 489-508.

Panos, R. & Astin, A. (1968). Attrition among college students. *American Educational Research Journal, 5,* 57-72.

Pantages, T.J. & Creedon, C.F. (1978). Studies of college student attrition: 1955-1975. *Review of Educational Research, 48*(1), 49-101.

Pascarella, E.T. (1980). Student-faculty informal contact and college outcomes. *Review of Educational Research, 50,* 545-95.

Pascarella, E.T. (Ed.) (1982). *Studying student attrition.* San-Francisco: Jossey-Bass.

Pascarella, E. & Chapman, D. (1983). A multiinstitutional, path analytic validation of Tinto's model of college withdrawal. *American Educational Research Journal, 20*(1), 87-102.

Pascarella, E.T. & Terenzini, P.T. (1977). Patterns of student faculty informal interaction beyond the classroom and voluntary freshman attrition. *Journal of Higher Education, 48,* 540-552.

Pascarella, E.T. & Terenzini, P.T. (1979). Interaction effects in Spady's and Tinto's conceptual models of college dropout. *Sociology of Education, 52,* 197-210.

Pascarella, E.T. & Terenzini, P.T. (1980). Predicting freshman persistence and dropout decisions from a theoretical model. *Journal of Higher Education, 51,* 60-75.

Perry, W.G. (1970). *Forms of intellectual and ethical development in the college years.* New York: Holt, Rinehart and Winston.

Perry, W.G. (1988). Different worlds in the same classroom. In P. Ramsden (Ed.), *Improving learning: New perspectives.* London: Kogan Page.

Pfundt, H. & Druit, R. (1985). *Bibliography: Students' alternative frameworks and science education.* Kiel, West Germany: Institut fur die Padogogik der Naturwissenschaften.

Powell, R., Conway, C. & Ross, L. (1990). Effects of student predisposing characteristics on student success. *Journal of Distance Education* 5(1), 5-19.

Pratt, D.D. (1984). Andragogical assumptions: Some counter-intuitive logic. *Proceedings of the Adult Education Research Conference,* No. 25. Raleigh: North Carolina State University.

Price, J.L. & Mueller, C.W. (1981). A causal model of turnover for nurses. *Academy of Management Journal, 24,* 543-565.

Ramsden, P. (1984). The context of learning. In F. Marton, D. Hounsell & N. Entwistle (Eds.), *The experience of learning.* Edinburgh: Scottish Academic Press.

Ramsden, P. (1987). Improving teaching and learning in higher education: The case for a relational perspective. *Studies in Higher Education, 12*(3), 275-286.

Ramsden, P. (Ed.) (1988). *Improving learning: New perspectives.* London: Kogan Page.

Ramsden, P., Beswick, D. & Bowden, J. (1986). Effects of learning skills interventions on first year university students' learning. *Human Learning, 5,* 151-164.

Ramsden, P. & Entwistle, N.J. (1981). Effects of academic departments on students' approaches to studying. *British Journal of Educational Psychology, 51,* 368-383.

Rayner, T.E. & Schmid, R. (1985). *Identification of potential distance learning drop-outs.* Montreal: Institute of Canadian Bankers.

Redding, N.P. & Dowling, W.D. (1992). Rites of passage among women reentering higher education. *Adult Education Quarterly, 42*(4), 221-236.

Reigeluth, C.M. (1979). In search of a better way to organize instruction: The elaboration theory. *Journal of Instructional Development*, 2(3), 8-15.

Reigeluth, C.M. (Ed.) (1983). *Instructional-design theories and models: An overview of their current status*. Hillsdale, NJ: Lawrence Erlbaum.

Reigeluth, C.M. (1989). Educational technology at the crossroads: New mindsets and new directions. *Educational Technology Research and Development*, 37 (1), 67-80.

Reigeluth, C.M. (1992). Elaborating the elaboration theory. *Educational Technology Research and Development*, 40(3), 80-86.

Reigeluth, C.M. & Merrill, M.D.(1979). Classes of instructional variables. *Educational Technology*, 19(3), 5-24.

Reigeluth, C.M., Merrill, M.D., Wilson, B.G. & Spiller, R.T. (1980). The elaboration theory of instruction: A model for sequencing and synthesizing instruction. *Instructional Science, 9*, 195-219.

Reigeluth, C.M. & Stein, F.S. (1983). The elaboration theory of instruction. In C.M. Reigeluth (Ed.), *Instructional-design theories and models: An overview of their current status*. Hillsdale, NJ: Lawrence Erlbaum.

Rekkedal, T. (1972). Correspondence studies–recruitment, achievement and discontinuation. *Epistolodidaktika, 2*, 3-38.

Rekkedal, T. (1973). *The written assignments in correspondence education. Effects of reducing turn-around time. An experimental study*. Oslo: NKI-skolen Undervisningssentrum.

Rekkedal, T. (1985) *Introducing the personal tutor/counsellor in the system of distance education*. Stabekk, Norway: NKI-skolen.

Roberts, D., Boyton, B., Buete, S. & Dawson, D. (1991). Applying Kember's linear-process model to distance education at Charles Sturt University-Riverina. *Distance Education, 12*(1), 54-84.

Rogers, C. (1969). *Freedom to learn*. Columbus, OH: Charles E. Merrill.

Rootman, I. (1972). Voluntary withdrawal from a total adult socialization organization: A model. *Sociology of Education, 45*, 258-270.

Roth, K. & Anderson, C. (1988). Promoting conceptual change learning from science textbooks. In P. Ramsden (Ed.), *Improving learning: New perspectives*. London: Kogan Page.

Rothkopf, E.Z. (1965). Some theoretical and experimental approaches to problems in written instruction. In J.D. Krumboltz (Ed.), *Learning and the educational process*. Chicago: Rand McNally.

Rowntree, D. (1986). *Teaching through self instruction: A practical handbook for course developers*. London: Kogan Page.

Rumble, G. (1982a) The Univerdad Nacional Abierta, Venezuela. In G. Rumble & K. Harry (Eds.), *The distance teaching universities*. London: Croom Helm.

Rumble, G. (1982b) The Univerdad Estatal a Distancia, Costa Rica. In G. Rumble & K. Harry (Eds.), *The distance teaching universities*. London: Croom Helm.

Rumble, G. (1989). Open learning, distance learning and the misuse of language. *Open Learning*, 4(2), 28-36.

Rutter, D.R. & Robinson, B. (1981). An experimental analysis of teaching by telephone: Theoretical and practical implications for social psychology. In G.M. Stephenson & J. Davis (Eds.), *Progress in applied social psychology*, vol. 1. New York: John Wiley & Sons.

Scales, K. (1984). A study of the relationship between telephone contact and persistence. *Distance Education*, 5(2), 268-276.

Schoenfield, A.H. (1992). Radical constructivism and the pragmatics of instruction. *Journal of Research in Mathematics Education*, 23, 290-295.

Schuell, T.J. (1986). Cognitive conceptions of learning. *Review of Educational Research*, 56 (4), 411-436.

Schuemer, R. & Strohlein, G. (1991). Diagnosis and therapy: Theoretical and methodological aspects of drop-out research. *Proceedings of the International Symposium on Distance Education in Theory and Practice*, Institute for Distance Education Research of the FernUniversitaet (ZIFF), September 1990.

Seels, B. (Ed.) (in press). *Instructional design fundamentals: A reconsideration*. Englewood Cliffs, NJ: Educational Technology Publications.

Sewart, D. (1981). Distance teaching: A contradiction in terms? *Teaching at a Distance*, 19, 8-18.

Sewell, W. & Shah, V. (1967). Socio-economic status, intelligence, and the attainment of higher education. *Sociology of Education*, 40, 1-23.

Shale, D.G. (1982) Attrition: A case study. In J.S. Daniel, M.A. Stroud & J.R. Thompson (Eds.), *Learning at a distance: A world perspective*. Edmonton: Athabasca University/ICDE.

Sheath, H.C. (1965). *External studies, the first ten years 1955-1964.* Armidale: The University of New England.

Shott, M. (1985). Teaching physics at a distance. *Distance Education,* 6(1), 102-127.

Smith, P. & Kelly, M. (Eds.) (1987). *Distance education and the mainstream.* Beckenham, Kent: Croom Helm.

Smith, P.J. (1976). More open admission policies: Some effects and some possibilities in an Australian case. *Epistolodidaktika,* 2, 46-56.

Smith, P.J. (1979). *Performance and attrition in the wake of expanded admission. A comparison of external students with part time and full time on-campus students.* Paper presented at the 5th biennial general meeting of the Australian and South Pacific External Studies Association, Perth.

Snedecor, G.W. & Cochran, W.G. (1967). *Statistical methods.* Ames, Iowa: Iowa State University Press.

Spady, W. (1970). Dropouts from higher education: An interdisciplinary review and synthesis. *Interchange,* 1, 64-85

Spady, W. (1971). Dropouts from higher education: Toward an empirical model. *Interchange,* 2, 38-62.

Spaeth, J. (1970). Occupational attainment among male college graduates. *American Journal of Sociology,* 4, 632-644.

Sparkes, J.J. (1989). Quality in engineering education. *Engineering Professors Conference Occasional Paper,* No. 1.

SPSS Inc. (1986). *SPSS-X users guide.* Chicago: SPSS Inc.

Store, R. & Chick, J. (1984). Reaching out in Queensland: A decentralised approach. In K. Smith (Ed.), *Diversity down under in distance education.* Toowoomba: Darling Downs Institute Press.

Store, R. & Osborne, B. (1979) Some factors affecting withdrawal of students from external courses: The experience of a small non-metropolitan college. *ASPESA Newsletter,* 5(2), 16-25.

Strike, K.A. & Posner, G.J. (1985). A conceptual change view of learning and understanding. In L.H.T. West & A.L. Pines (Eds.), *Cognitive structure and conceptual change.* New York: Academic Press.

Summerskill, J. (1962). Dropouts from college. In N. Sanford (Ed.), *The American college.* New York: John Wiley & Sons.

Sweet, R. (1986). Student dropout in distance education: An application of Tinto's model. *Distance Education,* 7(2), 201-213.

Taylor, E. (1984). Developing study skill. In E.S. Henderson & M.B. Nathenson (Eds.), *Independent learning in higher education*. Englewood Cliffs, NJ: Educational Technology Publications.

Taylor, J.C. & White, V.J. (1981). *Is any face-to-face contact necessary in distance education?* Paper presented to the ASPESA National Workshop, Adelaide.

Taylor, J.C. *et al.* (1986). Student persistence in distance education: A cross-cultural multi-institutional perspective. *Distance Education, 7*(1), 68-91.

Taylor, R. & Hanson, G. (1970). Interest and persistence. *Journal of Counselling Psychology*, 506-509.

Terenzini, P.T., Lorang, W.G. & Pascarella, E.T. (1981). Predicting freshman persistence and voluntary dropout decisions: A replication. *Research in Higher Education, 15*, 109-127.

Terenzini, P.T. & Pascarella, E.T. (1977). Voluntary freshman attrition and patterns of social and academic integration in a university: A test of a conceptual model. *Research in Higher Education, 6*, 25-43.

Terenzini, P.T. & Pascarella, E.T. (1978). The relation of students' precollege characteristics and freshman year experience to voluntary attrition. *Research in Higher Education, 9*, 347-366.

Thomas, P.R. & Bain, J.D. (1984). Contextual differences of learning approaches: The effects of assessments. *Human Learning, 3*, 227-240.

Thompson, G. (1984). The cognitive style of field-dependence as an explanatory construct in distance education drop-out. *Distance Education, 5*(2), 286-293.

Thorpe, M. (1987). Tutorial groups in open learning. In M. Thorpe & D. Grugeon (Eds.), *Open Learning for adults*. Harlow, Essex: Longman.

Thorpe, M. & Grugeon, D. (1987). Moving into open learning. In M. Thorpe & D. Grugeon (Eds.), *Open learning for adults*. Harlow, Essex: Longmans.

Thorpe, M. *et al.* (1986). The human dimension in open university study. *Open Learning, 1*(2), 14-20.

Tierney, W.G. (1992). An anthropological analysis of student participation in college. *Journal of Higher Education, 63*(6), 603-618.

Timmins, J.A. (1986). *Darling Downs Institute of Advanced Education regional liaison officer network.* Paper presented to Queensland state seminar, Australian and South Pacific External Studies Association, Brisbane.

Tinto, V. (1975). Drop-out from higher education: A theoretical synthesis of recent research. *Review of Educational Research,* 45(1), 89-125.

Tinto, V. (1982). Limits of theory and practice in student attrition. *Research in Higher Education,* 26, 115-129.

Tinto, V. (1987). *Leaving college.* Chicago: University of Chicago Press.

Trent, J.W. & Medesker, L.L. (1968). *Beyond high school.* San Francisco: Jossey-Bass.

Van Gannep, A. (1960) *The rites of passage.* (M.B. Vizedom and G.L. Coffee, Trans.). Chicago: University of Chicago Press.

Walker, M. (1982). Local support for the local learner. J.S. Daniel, M.A. Stroud & J.R. Thompson (Eds.), *Learning at a distance: A world perspective.* Edmonton: Athabasca University/ICDE.

Waqa, M.V. (1984). The University of the South Pacific: Dimensions of time and space. In K. Smith (Ed.), *Diversity down under in distance education.* Toowoomba: Darling Downs Institute Press.

Watkins, D. & Hattie, J. (1981). The learning processes of Australian university students: Investigations of contextual and personological factors. *British Journal of Educational Psychology, 51,* 384-393

Watkins, D. & Hattie, J. (1985). A longitudinal study of the approaches to learning of Australian tertiary students. *Human Learning, 4,* 127-141.

Watts, M. & Bentley, D. (1987). Constructivism in the classroom: Enabling conceptual change by words and deeds. *British Educational Research Journal, 13*(2), 121-135.

Weiner, B. (1972). Attribution theory, achievement motivation and the educational process. *Review of Educational Research, 42,* 203-215.

Weiner, B. (Ed.) (1974). *Achievement motivation and attribution theory.* Morristown, NJ: General Learning Press.

Wenestam, C-G. (1978). Horisontalisering [Horizontalization]. Ett satt att missuppfatta det man laser. *Rapporter från Pedagogiska Institutionen, Goteborgs universitet,* nr 157.

West, L. (1988). Implications of recent research for improving secondary school science learning. In P. Ramsden (Ed.), *Improving learning: New perspectives.* London: Kogan Page.

West, L.H.T. & Pines, A.L. (Eds.) (1985). *Cognitive structure and conceptual change.* New York: Academic Press.

West, L.H.T., Fensham, P.J. & Garrard, J.E. (1985). Describing the cognitive structures of learners following instruction in chemistry. In L.H.T. West & A.L. Pines (Eds.), *Cognitive structure and conceptual change.* New York: Academic Press.

White, B. & Horwitz, P. (1988). Computer microworlds and conceptual change: A new approach to science education. In P. Ramsden (Ed.), *Improving learning: New perspectives.* London: Kogan Page.

Wichit Srisa-An (1984) Evaluation of higher distance education results: The case of Sukhothai Thammathirat Open University of Thailand. In *Evaluation of higher distance education results.* Madrid: Universidad Nacional de Educacion a Distancia.

Williams, E. & Chapanis, A. (1976). A review of psychological research comparing communications media. In *The Status of the Telephone in Education,* Proceedings of the 2nd Annual International Telephony Conference, Wisconsin.

Williams, I. & Gillard, G. (1986). Improving satellite tutorials at the University of the South Pacific. *Distance Education, 7*(2), 261-274.

Wilson, B. & Cole, P. (1992). A critical review of elaboration theory. *Educational Technology Research and Development, 40*(3), 63-79.

Woodley, A. (1987). Understanding adult student drop-out. In M. Thorpe & D. Grugeon (Eds.). *Open learning for adults.* Harlow, Essex: Longman.

Woodley, A. & McIntosh, N.E. (1980). *The door stood open—An evaluation of the open university younger students pilot scheme.* Sussex: The Falmer Press.

Woodley, A. & Parlett, M. (1983). Student drop-out. *Teaching at a Distance, 24,* 2-23.

Woodley, A., Thompson, M. & Cowan J. (1992). Factors affecting non-completion rates in Scottish universities. *Interchange, 13,* 1-5.

Zajkowski, M.E. (1993). Business students learning at a distance: One form of pre-enrollment counselling and its effect on retention. *Distance Education, 14*(2), 331-353.

Glossary

The glossary contains brief definitions of the main components of the model and important concepts on which the model is based. Most of the terms included in the glossary apply to reasonably complex concepts so the succinct definitions may not always do full justice. For this reason a chapter is indicated at the end of each definition where the concept is discussed more fully.

Academic failure—Used here to classify those shown in institutional records as having failed to pass their course or program of study. In most institutions these figures also include informal withdrawals. (Chapter 2)

Academic integration—Integration considers the extent to which students become incorporated into the fabric of college society. In the model everything touching on the teaching and support environment is deemed to be part of the academic sphere. This then comprises all elements within the study package. It encompasses all contacts, face-to-face or by various media, with faculty, administrators and fellow students whether for study, administrative or social purposes. (Chapters 4 and 9)

Adult student—One aged 25 or over on entry to a course. (Chapter 1)

Andragogy—A set of assumptions about the learning of adults which are perhaps best interpreted as a definition of best practice in the teaching of adults. (Chapter 1)

Attrition—In most instances is used as a synonym for drop-out. (Chapter 2)

Collective affiliation— A student's sense of belonging in a course or to an institution. (Chapters 3 and 4)

Conceptions—How students perceive and understand important phenomena in their discipline. (Chapter 13)

Deep approach—Deep approach is the approach to study adopted by those who seek the underlying meaning of what they read and actively relate it to their own experience and needs. (Chapter 9)

Distance education—A full definition of distance education is given in Chapter 1. The most important element of this definition is seen as being the physical separation between teacher and learner for most of the instruction. (Chapter 1)

Distractions— A sub-scale of external attribution which attributes lack of application to study tasks to competing demands from family, employers and friends. It is indicative of a lack of social integration between academic demands and daily life. (Chapter 8)

Drop-out—Anyone who enrolls in a program and does not eventually complete it is normally classified as a drop-out. This broad interpretation of drop-out masks a wide variety of paths into and out of programs. (Chapter 2 and Figure 2-1)

Enrollment encouragement—A component of the social integration scale which examines the extent to which the employer, family and friends supported the student's decision to enroll in the course. Such initial support has an important bearing upon goal commitment. (Chapter 7)

Events hinder study—A sub-component of external attribution which examines the way in which happenings not foreseen at the time of enrollment influence the cost-benefit analysis between continuing and ceasing study. (Chapter 8)

External attribution—Drop-outs tend to attribute their withdrawal to factors outside their control so as to salvage some self-esteem. (Chapter 8)

Extrinsic motivation—That provided by rewards external to the course such as increased promotion opportunities or pay rises if a course is passed. (Chapter 9)

Family environment— A sub-scale of social integration which determines whether a warm supporting environment exists within the family unit. (Chapter 7)

Formal withdrawal—Students who cease to study in a program subsequent to completing an institution's formal withdrawal process. (Chapter 2)

GPA—Grade point average. (Chapter 10)

Informal withdrawal—Students who cease to study in a program without completing the formal withdrawal procedures. (Chapter 2)

Insufficient time—A sub-component of external attribution, included as the most common reason given for drop-out in autopsy reports and indicating a failure to come to terms with competing priorities. (Chapter 8)

Intrinsic motivation—Intrinsic motivation is manifest by those who are interested in their subject for its own sake. (Chapter 13)

Language ability—A sub-scale of external attribution, which gives a measure of the students' ability in the language of instruction. (Chapter 9)

Negative course evaluation—A sub-scale of external attribution which examines course materials, tutoring, assignment marking and administration, resulting in student feedback which is negative. (Chapter 9)

Normative congruence—In this context, congruence occurs if a student's intellectual beliefs and values are consistent with the expectations of the college and its faculty. (Chapters 3 and 4)

Open learning—There is no simple widely agreed definition of open learning. Courses are usually assessed for their degree of openness on a number of criteria concerned with access and student-centered learning. (Chapter 1)

Part-time student—A student who does not enroll for the full load of a program normally because he or she is prevented from doing so due to significant commitments to work, family and social lives in addition to his or her role as a part-time student. (Chapter 1)

Path analysis—A statistical technique used to test the fit of variables to a hypothesized model. (Chapter 11)

Pedagogy—In conventional usage pedagogy often refers to the science of teaching in a very general sense. Knowles restricts its applicability to the teaching of adolescents and assumes a highly teacher-centered model of adolescent teaching. (Chapter 1).

Persistence—The opposite to attrition and drop-out. The proportion of an enrolled cohort who do complete a program. (Chapter 2)

Positive course evaluation—A sub-component of academic integration meaning that there has been positive student feedback on course materials, tutoring, assignment marking and administration. (Chapter 9)

Reading habit—A sub-scale of academic integration which examines the extent to which students enjoy reading and read widely. (Chapter 9)

Social integration—Social integration refers to the degree to which the student is able to integrate the demands of part-time study with the continuing commitments of work, family and social life. (Chapters 4, 7 and 8)

Student progress—Used in this book as a composite measure of persistence and academic achievement, which is normally reflected by awarded grades. (Chapter 2)

Study encouragement—A component of the social integration scale which considers the degree of cooperation and moral support the student receives when actually studying. (Chapter 7)

Surface approach—The approach adopted by students who focus on the surface aspects of a text. They tend to concentrate on trying to rote-learn factual details which they presume will be relevant to examination questions. (Chapter 9)

Author Index

Subject Index